ASIYE'S STORY

Asiye Guzel

ASIYE'S STORY

Translated from the Turkish by
Richard McKane

SAQI

*To all those who have lost their lives
from torture in the struggle for freedom*

British Library Cataloguing-in-Publication Data
A catalogue record for this book is available from the
British Library

ISBN 0 86356 194 2

This edition published 2003 by Saqi Books

Saqi Books
26 Westbourne Grove
London W2 5RH
www.saqibooks.com

Foreword

by Helen Bamber OBE

Asiye's story makes difficult but compelling reading. Her description of torture and rape and the manipulation of a judicial system may be beyond the comprehension of those who know little of what goes on in Turkish police stations and Turkish prisons. But Asiye speaks for countless women, young and old, who have stood naked, blindfolded before those without pity or remorse, to be taunted, tortured with suspension and electric shocks and to be raped. In less than one day, hope for a future, a family life, for the joy of motherhood, to feel, to enjoy — all can be crushed in less than one day.

Some women who, like Asiye, have found the courage to speak out publicly against the perpetrators of these outrageous acts, now face a charge of slandering the state. Asiye's own future hangs in the balance. But she has achieved much in her writing; for she has been able to put into words the fear, the pain and the loneliness of a struggle to not only face the oppressors but to accept the irrevocable damage that has been done whilst not surrendering to the suffering.

Asiye was born and lived in a country in which torture is endemic and much injustice exists. She wanted change so that a humane society could emerge: for this she was tortured and raped. My question is always the same when I meet a woman who has endured and suffered as Asiye has. What is my society prepared to do about such a stain on the conscience of the world? And would we welcome the Asiyes of the world if they sought refuge in our country in fear of further torture and rape?

Since I started to write this comment, Asiye has been forced to seek asylum in a European country. She now faces what many call the defeat of exile. Recovery from such physical hardship will take time, and reconciliation to a life remote from the one of her dream may take longer. But Asiye's courage and her words should be a constant inspiration to those of us who try to work for change.

February 2003

Preface to the English Edition

In the days when I was beginning to write my book, a very dear friend said to me: 'Your book will be published in many countries in the world and in many languages; you must believe this, because the pain you have been through is a universal one and people cannot ignore the documentation of it.' When she said this, I looked at my friend in shock and with slight amusement. It is now three years since my book came out and I have been asked to write this preface for the English edition. It is only seven months since I have put distance between myself and the thick walls of prison. A period in my life has ended, and a new one begun.

I am in a different country, forced to live far away from the country and people I love. On 16 October 2002, I was given a twelve-and-a-half-year prison sentence in the case that had been brought against me. If I attempt to return to Turkey, I will be incarcerated again.

During my five and a half years in prison I came to understand life anew, from many angles. In a way, I tried to value my prison years as a school. But it was a very hard education. I discovered the meaning of close friendship, love, pain, resistance and the wonderful power of the human presence; I witnessed again and again that there is nothing that people cannot do if they really want to.

It is not easy for me to tell of my experiences, especially after the night of 19 December 2002, when the operation was launched to implement 'F-Type' prisons along with the policy of isolation called 'Return to Life'. (The latter was an operation carried out in many prisons, where police brutally stormed the wards where prisoners were on hunger strikes. The inmates were objecting to the F-Type prisons, whereby political prisoners were to be held in ones or twos rather than in wards.) From then on a chapter was opened and a period begun in which I saw and experienced things the likes of which have not been documented anywhere. That night more than twenty people lost their lives by being burnt, gassed and shot by the weapons of the state. In protest against this, there were people who set themselves alight; and in a hunger strike to the death that ensued nearly 100 people died, up to the time I was set free. Hundreds of others on hunger strikes were overcome by Wernicke-Korsakoff syndrome (caused by long-term malnutrition) and left crippled – including my husband, who was on a hunger strike for 358 days and is still in prison.

Today hundreds of people are still struggling to recover,

unaware of the future, unaware of the moment they are living in, having forgotten the past, but still breathing and living. This is a result of policies decided by the Turkish state. Thirteen people on my ward, in the five years we were together, willingly went on hunger strikes to the death. At that time there was no other way to oppose the isolation cells. Out of those thirteen, a very dear friend lost her life and the rest were left crippled. In my last year and a half in prison, apart from my own suffering, I witnessed this pain and heroism on a massive scale. This was a gruelling experience. I watched my fellow inmates march towards death unhesitatingly, without complaining, for the right only to live in conditions worthy of human beings. Their willpower was formidable, as they knew their actions would end in death and indescribable suffering, their bodies melting away day after day.

The shame of Turkey is its statewide endorsement of torture, and not just restricted to police stations and security buildings. As a policy it is widespread, and continues despite all the announcements made by authorities about changing laws. There is no doubt in my mind that I would have preferred not to have written this book. It was forced upon me. Sexual violence against women is only one example of the products of the torture machine. Rape, one of the greatest crimes against humanity, continues to be committed, and on the street and at home it is defended and categorised as an ordinary crime. In the torture rooms it becomes a fascist revenge crime, and in the capitalist- imperialist invasions, it is a war crime against the oppressed.

In Turkey, the practice of rape in custody is widespread. In Kurdistan, women have experienced this form of torture even more savagely, and it is common in the big cities. There are now court cases brought on the charge of rape, but under the influence of social values in Turkey very few victims are able to make it to the trials. Notifications of wrongdoing are rejected and the officers, the guilty parties, are free to return to their 'duties'. The suit that we tried to bring against the police torturers was rejected by all the official institutions, and when all the domestic legal avenues were closed, we took the case to the European Court of Human Rights. It is still being heard there.

It is not possible for me to forget what I have been through, though I have learned to live with and overcome the pain. I wish for a Turkey, a world, where people could live free of oppression and on equal terms, where women are not 'the second sex', where children wouldn't sleep rough and people wouldn't wander hungry on the streets, where torturers wouldn't exist. I believe all this can be brought about. Sooner or later humanity will achieve these great tomorrows, fragrant with freedom. I shall try to do all that is in my power to assist the struggle for human rights and democracy in the life I have left.

January 2003

Preface to the Turkish Edition

Life is so rich that it will broaden, and again and again make meaningless the boundaries of an individual's dreams. I call this thought to mind in the darkest nights, in the most hopeless moments, while trying to treat incurable wounds and when in greatest pain or joy. Life is so rich, so full of goals and beauty to die for. I recognise this richness and beauty with all my heart and mind. Finally, time is flowing. 'There is no way out/ my heart/ no other way/ we will survive these pains': I have never forgotten those lines from the poet Metin Demirtas, and when they are uttered I enter another time, another life, a time of discovery, of conquering new horizons and animating new thoughts. Yes, it is another climate, a country where this could be said (after Safak Taner): 'The friends gave the signal/ it's time/ in the shouts of the people/ a revolution will blossom like flags.'

Writing this book was a progression from a glacial climate to springtime. It was a very tense process. Soon after the courtroom announcement, it was suggested to me that I should write about my experiences. But I replied: 'It's not necessary. I'm not the only one who experienced this. There are people who went through much worse.' It didn't seem really necessary to me to write. The thought that such a work could be an effective weapon in the war against the torturers, and that it could pave the way to serious changes in peoples' consciousness, seemed to me nothing but a dream.

Despite all these negative thoughts, I decided to attempt to write. I began, but immediately gave up; I couldn't get past the first page. I had to convince myself. I struggled to continue later, on various occasions, but each time I left the writing half-finished, telling myself: 'I can't do it, can't describe, can't write.' Gradually, I began to persuade myself of the necessity of sharing this task, and the writing process developed as a result of arguments and discussions with my comrades. But this was during a period when my mental state was choked with nightmares. I was being treated by doctors; I hurled down the pen and paper and got up so many times after I had sat down at the table to write. I abandoned it, and didn't regard it as helping me make psychological progress. I took writing off my agenda for a long time.

But the process did go forward. There were intense, agonising reckonings, confrontations, facing up to realities and struggles of will, which resulted in changes in my life, feelings and thoughts. I ended by believing it was vital to share and write. I began rather irritably. I could have abandoned it halfway with an 'I can't do it', because it's one thing to tell one's story to someone and a completely different thing to write it down.

I began writing on 21 February without a detailed plan in mind. Trying not to let that worry me, I continued writing, remembering day after day and time after time the incidents and my inner life during those periods. This time I didn't experience any negative reactions, as in the previous attempts I'd made. I tried to write as though talking to a friend or comrade, which proved very useful to me. The process of writing opened the way for me to examine myself, and gave me the opportunity to understand my feelings and thoughts more consciously. When I took myself in hand I managed to look at my reality with different eyes. Sadness, tears, joy, laughter and anger all brought with them a great ease and calm.

It was a very important battle and I had won.

My writings eventually came back to me as a book, and when I first held it in my hands I felt intense and mixed feelings: excitement, enthusiasm, hope and even a little fear. People, outside my comrades and close circle would know and learn about what I felt and thought, what I had experienced and how I had experienced it. The way could be opened to negative public response, to angry words. But I was certain of one important result: especially among women, rape and sexual assault would be discussed and argued over.

These subjects were regarded as taboo, and went undiscussed; no attempts were made to understand them, even among revolutionaries. 'It's no different from other tortures'; 'They're the state and they do it': these were the sickening clichés that were accepted in revolutionary democratic circles. Rape passed for a normal form of torture.

I do accept that, in essence, it is no different from other tortures inflicted by the state. Assault by rape has the same aims and intentions as suspension by the arms or electric shock: to reduce a someone to a pulp; to throw them into total loneliness; to depersonalise them; to strip people of ideals and thoughts. But in Turkish society, which has predominantly retrogressive feudal values, rape – as far as women are concerned – has another meaning. It must be accepted that it is not easy for women who have grown up under retrogressive feudal terms to cast off their conditioning, even women who become revolutionaries.

Despite the fact that in recent years rape in custody has been increasing, it is a reality that those who have been raped rarely disclose the fact. If there is no difference between rape and other forms of torture, why do those who have experienced it hide it, while speaking easily of suspension, shock treatments, beatings, and so on? Why does it leave a person so especially damaged?

Will there arise an awareness of the necessity for a special campaign against rape and sexual assault? Undoubtedly there are women who have been exposed to this torture who are demanding retribution from the torturers, women who have not been defeated and who are speaking out in opposition to it. Unfortunately, however, they do not make up a majority.

Such a special campaign does exist in Turkey, and I wish to thank the Congress Against Rape and Sexual Assault in Custody (held in Istanbul) and all the people who make it work and give it their support with their labour and hearts, and to the EKB (Female Workers' Union), who organise it. The Congress is on the front lines against torture, sexual harassment and rape. It is vital for people to demand retribution from a state where torture and rape are matters of policy.

The Congress has a special importance and meaning for me, and marked a turning point in my life, as did coming to Kirklareli, the court hearing, the medical treatment and the book. It is the start of a new period and the end of an almost three-and-a-half-year process. I don't know how to express this better than to say that I have finally banished the feelings that were murdering me and annihilating me as a socialist and a woman. I am ready to fight with whatever resurfaces in my consciousness, whatever I've left missing or forgotten or thrown out. I'll continue to experience nightmares from time to time; the doctors have told me this, and perhaps there is even a scientific basis for them. But I am fighting to stop. Will I forget the past or dismiss it as nothing? Definitely not. From time to time I get a dull ache that is not the result of torture. It emerges as a thought: 'I could have behaved differently, resisted more.' Women are conditioned by society to form such notions, which are wholly inappropriate to the situation of rape. This false psychology, these sham values, put my identity as a socialist and human being under siege. The dull ache makes itself felt despite the fact that I now see these feelings for what they are.

What I have gained is the wish for a more powerful struggle, as well as new desire, passion, and a joy of life. I have fallen in love again with life, with people and the world, more consciously than before. I have learned what I can do with my willpower, my hopes for the future and my belief in big and happy tomorrows; I would give justice to life. I know I have only to work and be patient. Writing this book, I had to mould many of my feelings. I knew there were many things missing, but once I set out on this road there was to be no stopping. One phase had ended, and this new one became a conscious period of struggle and integration, more intense and difficult, a period which enveloped my flesh and bones in the thoughts and feelings leaping out.

And fear! I came to perceive the weight of its heavy burden on my shoulders. The declarations of the women at the Congress, all the letters I received, reminded me of what I had to do and how far I could take it. I experienced the same feelings with each and every woman who came out in public. I could not fall back, and above all I could not rest with my shame. This frightened me. I didn't fear the unknown but rather the known, and was conscious of a heavy duty and the fear I harboured of not carrying it out, not being worthy of it. The fear reminded me that I had to work and become stronger. At one point I was possessed by this fear and uncertainty of the future. What would I do when I came out of prison? There was no definite answer to that: it was veiled in mist. Perhaps it was the urgency that made me afraid, or the knowledge that my future was in my hands, that it wasn't uncertain and that I could design it as I liked.

For some time a wish to take revenge on the torturers governed me intensely. But confronting them now, standing on my own two feet, is in itself revenge: 'You couldn't achieve what you wanted. I am on my feet again and fighting you. You won't ever defeat me again.' Shouting this is revenge. I learned that one must begin by passing through feelings of revenge and hatred.

After the book came out, many things changed in my life. I became certain of the rightness of what I had done, especially when shortly afterwards responses came in, both positive and negative. People started arguing and discussing, questioning themselves and bringing themselves to account – women and men alike. I received many messages and letters from all sections of the community. People told of their experiences, their feelings, in a very open way. Many of their experiences had been hidden, never spoken of before then.

In prison I became armoured with the deep belief that people can overcome obstacles if they really want to; above all, I had an unshakeable faith in the future. My faith in myself and in the road I had taken was strengthened. As my life flowed on before me I tried to will the flow and give it direction, to stop being a spectator and make decisions, to develop willpower and stubbornness. On a daily basis I made practical plans for ordering the future, set goals, dreamed dreams and strove to win back the moral values I had lost. I tried to take notice of the changes in feeling and thought that I was experiencing. Day by day, month by month, I tried to be conscious of the changes within me and to attain stability. I made an insistent and stubborn progress, trying to understand and not be afraid of criticising myself. Life changes all the time. Death is natural; so is the counterpoint of old and new, and the struggle of people to become fully human. I know that I am missing qualities and have weaknesses, but the most important thing is that I am not afraid of them. I struggle with them, I overcome them. I bravely face them, trying to reach my goal and avoid being tied down.

The climate in which I live today is different. It carries the colours of the rainbow. It is a rich world where all human values and goals are embraced. It gives happiness and joy. I am inside four walls, but the world is in my palms. The world is mine, you see, life is mine. And yet more difficult days are waiting for me. Every day my hatred and anger grow in my heart at this system and its protectors, drenched in blood from top to bottom. But my belief and hope for those great tomorrows grow greater, fragrant with freedom. I am not afraid to live crazily. My hope, my love of life, my stubbornness, my resistance are all like the wide world. I can do much more; I have this power. I am an active part of the great humanity that will conquer the world. I carry this honour, this happiness.

Yes, it is a happy climate, beautiful as the rainbow. It is a climate where bravery, hope and stubbornness will blossom and inevitably overcome the pain, the difficulties, the weaknesses. 'The friends gave the signal/ it's time/ in the cries of the people/ a revolution will blossom like flags.' These lines bring light.

October 2000

Introduction

Can you find your way on a starless night? Even if you have studied the road, can you walk it without going astray? How lucky you are if you can find it without hesitation. But you've got serious problems if you get stuck, stumble, fall without the possibility of getting up. Everyone can find the road on a night when the stars are shining, but what if there aren't any stars, or if your heart is so darkened you can't see them. You stumble, fall, try to get up again, but you are stunned with pain. All your organs are wounds that won't close. You can't see the outstretched hands trying to pull you out of the darkness, because you are swiftly flowing towards extinction. You won't find or see the stars. You separate life into colours: you give a name to every one, but you won't find a colour for this. You'll cry, cry and cry again. Nothing will change, relief would only be temporary. You can't solve the problem or even take a step.

In life there are obvious turning points. There are days when your dreams of the future are recognised and nights when you nurture the hope for those days. They are blood red; your tiniest cells burn and roast you. You are born again every morning. Each step of the way is significant. You live your life to the full. You feel life in every cell of your body. Then one day you realise that you love and are in love. This is another colour for you. You give it the name of green and blue. It's deep as the sea and green as a plane tree that is starting to put out shoots. You hide it in a corner of your heart. And one day you roll down to the bottom of the abyss. You throw yourself down and ask: 'Does life go this far?' You can't find a colour for this. There is no white in the long, cold days; nature colours itself grey and black. You know, however, that the future holds all the shades of green and blue. This is an unchangeable law of nature. But your life is now something else. Red, blue, green, black, grey – you will erase all these colours. A huge emptiness remains in your head. Long, dark nights follow, one after another. Your experience is not a nightmare. When you think it is and deceive yourself, you smash harshly into reality. And every time you are thrown to the ground again. Your knees can't hold you up. In a moment your life starts flowing in the opposite direction to the one that you want. The current is so strong, you have no strength to stop it. Monsters in human form try to take the colours from your hands.

A small, square room with a steel cupboard and a dirty, bare table. Walls painted white, a white that reflects nothing beautiful or good or pure. The only presence is the emptiness of the moment when you rolled down into the abyss. The floor is covered with a carpet, but the colour it had when laid has faded. There are two brown armchairs and a couple of windows. You can sleep hunched on the chairs by drawing them together. If you open your eyes and raise your head slightly you can see the sky. But the sky is not the same one you saw two days before. You're so tired, you just want to sleep. Despite the pains and aches you just want to sleep. You go in deep, but this is not sleep: it's worse than any nightmare. You can't remember how much time has gone by. You're still in the same room, on the same chair and lying in the same position. It's as though if you moved a tiny bit, reality would slap you in the face.

Every so often they check what you are doing. They don't leave you in peace so you can sleep. There is a thought that constricts your heart. You do your best to escape from it, but every time it comes back with even more force.

You drop swiftly to the bottom of the abyss. You can't find a branch to hold onto, neither can you see the stars. Where have they gone? They used to be so close. Were you ever this lonely? Were you ever this far from anyone? Did you ever love? Why did you throw yourself into the abyss? Or did you not notice that you were already at its edge …?

When you fell on the road, what was it that suddenly tripped you?

1

The weather was particularly good for February, no rain or snow. The sun played hide-and-seek with the clouds and reminded us that there was not long to go before spring. That day I returned home in the afternoon. We had spent the night at my husband's relatives. On my way home I did some shopping at the small supermarket for our evening meal. Everything seemed normal when I met the landlord as I opened the front door. I went up the stairs, key in hand, and just as I was about to open the flat door I noticed something strange. Before I could put the key in the lock, the door was suddenly flung open to reveal five or six people in the flat. At such times one's mind acts strangely and either starts to work very fast or exactly the opposite. When I saw the men, the first thing that came to mind was that they were robbers. But, of course, there would be no logic in their waiting for someone to come home after they'd finished their business. It didn't take me long to realise that these were policemen. Later, I laughed a lot whenever I recalled that moment of first encounter, when I had supposed that robbers had broken in.

I think the police also experienced an initial surprise. I didn't expect them and they didn't expect me. After the door was opened I stayed rooted to the spot, and so did they. But they soon recovered, and five or six of them jumped on me. I couldn't understand what had happened; I was shoved to the ground.

'Who are you? What are you looking for in our flat?' My questions received short, clear answers: kicks, slaps and swear words. Even while one is being beaten one can still manage to think. Under the rain of kicks and slaps I said to myself: 'The show's over.' This is what the police usually say to people when they take them into custody: 'The show's over, now talk.' Up until that day I had only read or heard this expression in books, newspapers or people's stories. They took my handbag and emptied out the contents. They said they were going to search me. I insisted that I wouldn't let them and requested that they find a woman officer to do it. The fiancée of our landlord lived on the top floor. When I insisted, they called her in as the 'woman officer'. When she came I was taken to another room in the flat. They ordered her to search me all over and they didn't neglect to throw in a threat: 'or else we'll take you in, too'.

She was shoved into the room behind me. The door was ajar. I asked them to shut it and they did not object. I asked the woman what had happened and when they had come, but she was too frightened and in too great a shock to give a straight answer.

I said: 'I won't take off my clothes, you'll have to search me like this.' She refused. I had no opportunity to persuade her as she immediately opened the door and told the men that I had refused to be searched. I was beaten again. They searched me forcibly. When they were done, they asked me my name. I said it was written on the identity card. Then one of them radioed somewhere and requested a car. I sat on a chair. They had turned the flat into chaos. The armchairs were all over the place; the cushions lay on the floor, and clothes and kitchen objects were scattered round the flat.

'I want to go to the toilet.'

'Just sit there, you can go later.'

They recorded the contents of my handbag on sheets of paper. I had the weekly magazine *Atilim* and the newspaper I had purchased from the newsagent on my way home. They wrote down, one by one, every item they had taken from my bag. They wanted me to sign. I said I wouldn't because I thought they would use the signed documents as prosecution evidence. They didn't insist.

I said again that I wanted to go to the toilet. This time they didn't object. I used the opportunity to glance at the other rooms in the flat on my way. Everywhere was the same, everything turned upside down; even the sink in the bathroom had been broken.

Just then a new person came into the room. That meant the car had arrived. They blindfolded me with my own scarf, and we went out of the house. Two men held onto my arms, and I was put into the car. Two men sat next to me, and we set off. I did not need to guess where I was being taken. After about fifteen minutes we came to the Security HQ building on Vatan Street. No one spoke a word for the whole journey.

A deep silence ensued. I could hear only the noise of the traffic. But I was talking to myself inside, thinking. How had they found the house? I had been the features editor of a socialist magazine, and worked for a socialist newspaper. As editor I had been arrested for an article and charged in the DGM (State Security Court). I had been in Bayrampasa prison for a short time, and after my release I had again started to work for a socialist newspaper. My husband and I had bought a new flat together; otherwise, if I were convicted in the case for which I was being prosecuted, and if they tracked me down, I would go to prison. No one knew where we were living, not even our families, and I used someone else's identity card since the police were still looking for me.

How did they find the house? This question tore at me, and I couldn't find an answer. But really it didn't make much sense to struggle with it. At the very least I had ten days in detention waiting for me. When I was a student at university I had been detained several times, and faced constant police pressure when working for newspapers. These events weren't unusual for me. I could have guessed that I would face them again. What I had been through at the flat were the first signs of this. In Turkey, if you are in possession of an 'opposition' identity card you always come up against the police. You can be taken into custody at any time, where you can be 'disappeared' or made to 'commit suicide'. Torture normally happens. As a result I wasn't in a state of shock or panic. On the way I had the opportunity to think about many other things too. Fifteen minutes is a very short time, but much can be fitted into even shorter spaces. My husband had no idea the flat had been raided, and I worried that when he came home in the evening he would go through what I had been through. I swore to myself and found myself praying that he wouldn't go home.

The human mind works very fast at such moments, because you don't think you're going to make it. All the organs of sense swing into action. You try to understand, catch and record the slightest details. You try to notice the changes around you, and all the time you are thinking. Many feelings arise and collide at once. Shock, resistance, hope, panic, fear, trust, uncertainty, anxiety; a whole series of uncontrollable feelings all flare up and compete in a terrible struggle with each other.

As far as I could tell, the car stopped outside the main door of the security building. Still no one spoke. They got me out of the car, and I realised from where my feet were treading that we were entering a building. We got into a lift and went up to what was probably the first or second floor. There was a strange silence, with not a sound except for our footsteps. We stopped somewhere, and they took the blindfold off. The light was blinding and dazzled my eyes for a moment. Where I was standing there was a sort of information desk like the kind found in big companies or hotel lobbies, except here instead of a placard reading 'Information' there was one marked 'MLKP-Team 3' (MLKP stands for the Marxist-Leninist Communist Party). The policemen who had brought me in handed me over to another person, signed some papers and went off. They took my handbag, shoelaces and belt, and wrote down all the possessions I had on me: watch, necklace, earrings, ring and money. They put them in a paper envelope. Later they gave me back my money, said they would return all my things to me and wanted me to sign the inventory sheet. I said I wouldn't sign, and they didn't insist much. They blindfolded me again – this time with a specially designed blindfold – and made it tighter than before. They took me by the arms, led me to another place and seated me in a chair.

For some time I was alone. No one came and went; there was only silence. I couldn't understand where I was or whether there were other people with me there. The enforced waiting was getting to me. In general, the police use such disorienting tactics for their own purposes and don't want to give their opponents any opportunity to think. My feelings began to collide again. This time anxiety put the most pressure on me: 'What would happen?' 'Who was here?' A flock of questions tormented me.

'I want to go to the toilet.'

Silence answered me. I said it a second time, and louder:

'I want to go to the toilet.'

Finally someone took my by the arm and said: 'Come on.'

We walked down a corridor. My blindfold was taken off in front of the toilet. It wasn't at all cold inside the building – the central heating must have been working well. I washed my hands and face thoroughly. My blindfold was put on again, and I taken back to the room and sat down in a chair. The silence was terrifying. There was no sound of footsteps. There can't have been anyone else in the room apart from me. Time passed quickly or slowly, I did not know. They had left me with myself. My feelings and thoughts continued to collide. Waiting was terrifying, silence was terrifying. I wanted whatever was going to happen to be over right then: let them do what they were going to do, just let there be no more sitting, no more of this waiting.

I couldn't work out how much time had passed. Once more someone took my arm and they took off the blindfold. My first impression was how clean the room was. I had been expecting a filthy room.

'Hey, Asiye, what's up?' one man said.

Then he continued: 'Why are you going around with someone else's identity card?'

'I am the features editor of the *Workers' Path* newspaper. Since I have been charged I carry this identity card.'

Then someone else came into the room. He was a tall man with fair hair.

'Do you take us for fools? What do you think these are that we found in your flat?'

'What do you mean?' I asked, looking at the various false documents that were laid out in front of me. I replied, 'There was nothing like that in our flat, they don't belong to us,' and as I said that I was slapped heavily by someone at my side. Was my jaw broken, I wondered?

'I want to get in touch with my lawyer and family.'

They laughed, and inside myself I wanted to laugh too. Such a request was truly comic for the situation I was in.

They put pen and paper on the table. One of the policemen, whom I presumed to be the leader, said: 'Sit down and write.' He put down a few identity cards and photos which he had in his hand, and pointed at them.

'Look, this one stays with you, this one comes and goes,' he started to say, and added: 'Don't mess with us, sit down and write.'

'I've nothing to write.'

'You know best.'

We were eye to eye and his didn't blink.

'Take her away and let her think a bit.'

They put on the blindfold tightly again. I was taken to what was probably the same place as before.

Again I was left with myself. The silence there became terrifying.

What time was it, I wondered. Had my husband come home? Why were they keeping me waiting? While I was lost in thought, wondering why they hadn't taken me to be tortured, a very strong hand suddenly grabbed my arm. I was taken again to the same room. They took off the blindfold.

'Nilgun, have you thought about it?

Nilgun ... But there wasn't anybody else in the room being held. He was talking to me, trying to disorient me.

'There's nothing to think about.'

'You'll be sorry, don't crush yourself, you'll see, you won't stand it ... '

'I've got nothing to say.'

'Leave them all, take this one first.'

They put on the blindfold again. I felt remarkably calm. We started to walk; the men were composed. It was obvious that they were used to doing this. They were as calm as I was.

'Take your top off and leave the rest on,' a voice shouted from behind.

We went up in the lift. There was a concrete floor in the

room to which I was taken. I could make this out from under the blindfold; there was nothing laid on the floor.

'Do you want to strip off or shall we do it?'

I stripped myself so they wouldn't touch my body.

I took off my scarf, sweater and T-shirt, and they sat me in a chair. I had never experienced suspension torture, but I guessed from what I had heard and read and what I knew of the procedures that it was now going to happen. They tied my arms to a wooden beam, and finally they finished. Hoopla, I was hanging. At first I said to myself: 'Hey, is this what they call hanging?' Initially one feels no pain at all. After some time, however, I started feeling sharp pains in my armpits. But they couldn't hold out for long, and let me down. My arms were numb, but I could still feel them. Two of the men were moving them around to make the numbness go away. Then they took off the rest of my clothes: my trousers, socks and underclothes. I wasn't in a position to oppose them. My arms were tied tightly behind me. They put them through the wooden beam. Suddenly I was up in the air again, and this time the pain was more acute. My attempts at breathing turned into another torture. My ribcage seemed to be bursting. There were no questions. No one talked, only voices that said: 'OK? Enough?' I was on the ground again. My arms had no sensation now. I was naked and my nakedness frightened me. I was ashamed – I, who felt uncomfortable if my skirt was a bit short, was naked in front of all these men. They had taken down all my defences. My husband came into my mind. I had to think of other things. I tried to sing a song to myself. Damn it, nothing came to mind. I had forgotten all the songs I ever knew. I tried to remember one line, one verse. On my mind was only my nakedness:

You're naked!

'That's OK, I knew that would happen.'

But you're naked. You've got nothing on.

I didn't know how many people there were in the room – I couldn't work it out from their voices and they didn't talk much.

You're naked!

'That's alright. They aren't human beings.'

I was sweating, sweating profusely as though bucket after bucket of water had been poured on me.

I had to think of something else.

You're naked in front of so many men, what are you thinking, you're naked! They can do to you whatever they want. Ask for your clothes.

I wasn't alone, someone inside me was speaking. We were fighting. Asiye had started fighting with Asiye.

You're naked. You've no protection.

'Let it be, I knew this would happen.'

But you're naked. Ask for your clothes, go on, ask for them. The men in the room are looking at you, ask for your clothes. Don't let them touch you, let them give you your clothes back. Don't ask for anything else, just your clothes. If they touch you, what will you say to your husband?

He knows that you could experience this. Both of you could have guessed this could happen. What could he say? But what if he would never want to be with you again, what if he felt disgusted with you?

If you don't ask for your clothes he will hate you. Go on, ask for your clothes.

I was in another world. I couldn't hear the questions, insults, swear words. They took me down again. My arms were not mine; I couldn't feel them.

Let them give me back my clothes, I pleaded silently. I didn't want anything else. On my mind were only my trousers, my sweater, my scarf. I was locked onto them.

More suspension followed.

Why don't you ask for your clothes, they are your armour, your shell. Ask for them!

'No, it'll all be over soon. They'll give them back then.'

They won't give them back if you don't ask for them. The quicker you put them on the better it'll be. You shouldn't stay naked any longer. Everyone is looking at you, examining you, observing you. Ask for your trousers.

Ask for your sweater.

Ask for your clothes.

Ask for them, time's passing, get on with it.

I had forgotten all the songs I knew and loved. I couldn't remember anyone's face, even those I loved most. There must be one, I thought, they couldn't be so distant ... I had to find a place to hold on to.

You're alone! There's no one to hold on to. Ask for your clothes. Ask for them, what more are you waiting for? They'll protect you.

I heard the door open. Some new person must have come in.

'Aren't you through yet? What are you trying to do? Let her down and lay her on the ground, the whore.'

Let her down and lay her on the ground?

I was let down from suspension. I couldn't stand, I couldn't feel my arms or control them. The pain was terrific. They threw me to the ground. After my head hit the ground, I felt the icy concrete. I was pouring sweat. I tried to use my arms to get on my feet, but I couldn't get through to them. I heard laughter and swear words. I tried to cover my nakedness, but couldn't. The thought came to mind that they would give me a beating there and then. I couldn't comprehend anything, I could only make out glimpses of their feet under my blindfold. I decided to give up trying to get to my feet, but tried to get my legs working. Their kicking stopped me. They held on tightly to my arms and legs. My efforts to struggle free were in vain. I tried to shout but no sound emerged.

'No, you can't do that – murder me, tear me apart but don't touch me. Don't dirty me, don't stain me!' I wanted to say. Everything was happening so fast, I was ready to go crazy. I felt a heaviness upon me. My teeth were clenched with the pain. I couldn't resist or move at all, not even get my mind to work. My throat was going to tear apart from screaming. My shouts, screams, my voice even seemed alien to me. The laughter and foul swearing never stopped. They were saying horrible things.

One of them said: 'Even your husband didn't manage this.'

When that horrible heaviness on me had finished its business, I felt frozen as water turned to ice. I was frozen like a mummy. Even my wish to die was taken away from me.

Suddenly everywhere went dark. There wasn't a single light. I was in the dark. A pitch black darkness like infinity. Everything, everyone had passed one by one to the other side of darkness. I was left alone. There was no one to stretch my hand out to, to hold it. I became aware that the heaviness on me had lifted. When it lifted it took my soul with it.

I couldn't recall my mother's face, or my father's, the faces of those I loved. I was rolling down into an abyss. I had been dirtied, I wouldn't be able to look anyone in the face, wouldn't be able to love, wouldn't be able to be a mother. I had nothing left to live for, they had taken everything away. I was lost in a vacuum.

When I came to I was lying in a chair; they had given back my clothes. I hugged them to me. There was no one in the room.

My eyes weren't blindfolded. I wanted to get to my feet but my body wouldn't allow it. I was like a corpse. I couldn't work out where reality began and ended. Someone came into the room and I tried to get up but couldn't.

'Do you want anything?'

I wanted some water, but no sound came out. I couldn't open my mouth.

He went out of the room. I just wanted to sleep, so that I wouldn't be here when I woke up ... so that I wasn't dirtied, so that I was clean. Fever was pressing on me from all sides but I was cold. I hugged my clothes to me even tighter.

I slept. I woke and I was still there. Curses, a thousand curses. This was a dream, a nightmare. Then why didn't it end? I had to sleep, to sleep, so this nightmare would end, so my loved ones would come and awaken me, saying, 'Wake up now, you've slept too long, that's enough.' I was waiting; why didn't anyone come? I was going crazy; this nightmare had no end. I had no concept of time. Two men came into the room. They held me under the arms and lifted me. I couldn't stand. My feet

and legs did not seem to belong to me – they were like a doll's
limbs. They held me by the arms and took me to another room.
They gave me a cigarette, but I had given up smoking. But how
I wanted one then! I accepted the cigarette, thinking that it
might help me get my head together. I took a couple of puffs
and my head started to spin. No one spoke. There was only
that accursed silence. How long had I been here? When did I
come here? I didn't know, I couldn't remember.

There was a piece of yellowish, cheap paper and a pen on
the table. They offered me the pen and I took it. What would I
do then, what would I write? I wanted to sleep, I couldn't stand
it, my eyelids felt they were lifting a weight of many tons.

And I started writing … But it was as though the hand that
wrote were not mine. I was watching it from another place, I
couldn't say 'don't write'. Even if I said it, I wouldn't have
heard it. I was so far from myself . If I had shouted out at the
top of my lungs, or screamed, no one would have heard me.

Everything was on the other side of the darkness. I was
completely alone; the other Asiye who had talked to me was
not there. She had upped and gone …

I had been taken into custody on the afternoon of 22
February 1997, and spent a total of thirteen days at the
Security HQ.

After I started writing they had all the control. Whatever
they said, I wrote. Whatever the stakes, this was the way to
ensure that they didn't touch me again. The swifter their
business with me got finished, the swifter I could be rescued
from their power. My sole purpose was to prevent them
touching me again.

I tried to erase from my memory that I had been raped. It

was very difficult, but from time to time I was successful. Strangely, I kept remembering either my childhood or my youngest brother. There were details I hadn't remembered for years: my mother taking us to the park; the times when my mother sometimes beat me; the times when my youngest brother was naughty. I used to laugh at these times and found it hard to control myself.

My little brother once strayed into a flock of sheep. He was three or four years old. We looked for him but couldn't find him. Suddenly we saw him up in the air in the middle of the flock, doing somersaults. He had managed to come across the only ram in the flock. We thought nothing of it, but the next day we took the precaution of taking him to the doctor: he had broken his collarbone. He was put in plaster from the lower back upwards, with just one arm dangling outside. Whenever we thought of this incident at home we went into fits of laughter. Once he had dived into a shop window on his bike ... It was as though I was reliving my childhood and many things relating to it came to my mind. Right up to the lycée – after that there was nothing. It was as though I hadn't existed after the lycée.

They didn't try to put much pressure on me after I had started to write what they wanted. Every so often they'd come and ask me about my husband: 'Surely a wife would know where her husband is?' and similar questions. At home there were letters from my husband to me, which I hadn't thrown out, and they had brought them to the Security HQ. From time to time they read them out beside me and laughed. All these activities seemed distant from me. Everything seemed to be happening outside me. I wasn't there. 'There's someone else there, that's not me,' I wanted to say. It was on the tip of my tongue, but I kept quiet. If I said something they would take my clothes again. I wouldn't allow them that.

I didn't miss any opportunity to sleep. It would definitely all be over when I woke. But every time I woke I found myself still there.

One day I was taken to the cells. There were three or four people in the cell where I was put. I was in no state to talk to anyone. I had to sleep right away. In the morning I was taken downstairs again. I just sat there and they didn't ask many questions.

The windows were, on the whole, kept closed and locked. They took the keys out of drawers or kept them in their pockets. I was thinking continuously of my childhood and laughing to myself. But an indescribable fear overwhelmed me inside. I kept reminding myself: 'You're asleep, when you wake up you won't be here, you must be calm.' I had a terrific wish to have a bath. I thought, 'I must have a bath, I need to get clean!' I knew that when I washed I'd get clean.

On the other hand, the idea of death pressured me: 'What more are you waiting for?' My childhood and death. I kept coming and going between these two. My eyes were on the windows. If I found one that was open I would let myself jump from it ... I was asleep anyway – then I'd wake up. A violent crash followed by an awakening. I tried to persuade myself that there was no other way of waking up. But the windows stayed locked. I had to find another way.

Finally I spotted an open window. One part of me was, terrifyingly, pushing me straight to it. My organs were still not in my control, they were like the insides of a toy. I took a few steps towards the window. If I stretched out my hand I could hold it. I wanted to wake up. A hand roughly and tightly took my arm and pushed me to the side. No! No way did I want them to touch me. No one must touch me. I pulled my scarf tightly round me in the corner into which I had been pushed.

After that day I was never left alone. There was always someone with me in the room I was in and I was far away from the windows. I had no concept of time. One evening they said my father was going to come.

My father used to come and pick me up when I was at secondary school, which was quite far from home. We got let out of school at 7.30 PM, and in the winter months it was dark. 'OK,' I would think, 'my father's coming to get me. Finally I'll be rescued from here!' I was happy to be going home with my father. I would make plans in my head: as soon as I got home I'd have a bath; my mother would prepare a meal, and after that I'd go straight to sleep in my bunk bed. In the morning everything would have returned to normal. How happy I was, how excited. He must come immediately; why was he late? He was never late, he was always at the school gate at 7.30 …

I was taken to another room. This was the room I had been taken to first . They didn't put the blindfold on anymore, and I could distinguish between the rooms. The door was slightly ajar. I heard footsteps.

Finally my father appeared. I wanted to throw myself into his arms and say: 'Let's go, you're late anyway, let's not lose time.' As my father came into the room, I felt something was holding me back. I wanted to embrace him, but I couldn't move. I was frozen. He took a few steps towards me; finally I was in his arms, but why was my father crying? He should not have been crying. I wanted to say, 'let's go home,' but I was afraid – the men were in the room and they would hinder us. I had to whisper it in my father's ear. I didn't want to leave him. He was asking me things; I gave answers. I was dying with frustration. Why were we waiting? Why weren't we going home? One of the policemen said: 'That's enough.' No, my father couldn't go and leave me here! I was his daughter, how could he leave me here! I hugged him tightly: no, I won't let you go.

It was not a trick of the light. It wasn't a dream. I hadn't been sleeping. When my father had gone out of the room I realised in a flash that what had just happened had been real. The moment I realised this I started sweating terribly and at the same time felt cold. Hopelessness, helplessness, panic and fear overwhelmed me. I was trembling inside. I was caught in a trap. No, if it weren't a dream, I would go mad. I kept repeating: 'It's a dream, a dream.' But reality was weighing down on me heavily. I had to find another way out.

'I wasn't raped. No one will look on me as dirty. I couldn't stand the pain of the suspension torture and I wrote what they wanted.' Yes, this lie would be easier to tolerate.

A few days later my mother came, and I was given permission to see her. I was calmer and believed more and more in the speculation that this was indeed reality. They had asked my mother to bring my personal effects from home, but she told them that she had nothing of mine. They decided that together we could go and get them from my home. My mother, two policemen and I went to the flat that had been raided. There was no one in the house, and the door hadn't yet been sealed. Everything was as it had been at the time of my arrest.

It was chaos – broken beds, blankets, books, cassettes, clothes were strewn all around; everything was on the floor. I put a few things together to take in a bag. I was like a machine, responding mechanically to perform various tasks. Whatever they said or asked, I did. 'Don't take that,' they said, and I left it. 'You'll need this,' they said and I took it. A doll that my husband had bought for me was lying on the floor. It caught my eye and I hesitated, but finally turned back and took it.

I came out of the flat with my mother beside me. One of the policemen felt he should issue me a warning: 'I'm a sharpshooter. I'm telling you this in case you're thinking of running away.'

Now I was staying in a room in the upper storey at Security HQ. The floor had a blue rug. There was a window – you could actually see outside. I looked at the buildings, roofs, people. My mother-in-law brought me money and some more things; they did not grant me permission to see her, and the things were brought to my room. They asked me to write a short note, which I gave to them and in which I said that I had received the things and I was well. I looked out of the window again. I saw my mother-in-law and her mother leaving the building. I waved to them, but they couldn't see me.

They had stopped trying to pressure me. They only took me down to take my statement, which they weren't hurrying to finish. Every day they took it a little further. When it was finished I signed it all. I also signed another lot of papers. It was of no importance to me what they were.

'You're feeling remorse,' I was told. 'You'll go to Kirklareli prison.'

...

'OK?'

'OK.' Why would I object? Everything was over. I didn't want to see or talk to anyone. I considered myself to be dead.

They said: 'Get ready, we're taking you to the doctor.'

The doctor asked if there were any scars from any beatings, and whether they had done this or that.

'No, they didn't do anything.'

'Get ready,' I was told afterwards. 'We're going to court. Don't forget, you feel remorse and you want to go to Kirklareli, that's what you'll say.'

Before I appeared before the prosecutor I was taken to a State Security Court judicial doctor. The scene was repeated there: 'No, they didn't do anything,' I said. 'They just gave me the suspension, that's all.'

From the policeman's look, I realised that I had said something I shouldn't have.

I said the same things in front of the prosecutor and judge. I repeated whatever I had signed my name to at the Security HQ. I just wanted everything to be over as soon as possible and to escape from the power of the police. I wasn't thinking of anything else. And I wanted to have a bath.

The judge asked: 'You want to go to Kirklareli, presumably.'

'Yes,' I said. I couldn't say no. I couldn't look at my own face, how could I look other people in the face? I didn't want to see anyone, I didn't want to see anyone I knew. I was so close to death, I didn't want to infect anyone. I was dirtied, humiliated, ashamed.

Finally it was over. First we went back to the Security HQ. The intention was to hold me there one more night, and then the next day I'd be taken to Kirklareli. One of the policemen, unfamiliar to me, opposed this, so we set off on the road to Kirklareli straight away.

I sat alone in the back seat, two policemen in the front. They spoke very little during the whole drive. Occasionally they asked questions about my husband. It was indeed days since I had said goodbye to him.

I was in endless darkness. There was no other 'I' talking to me any more: even she'd left me. Along the way I looked outside with empty eyes. What I saw – people, crowds, trees, sky – had no significance to me. It was as though I were the only person left in the huge world. There was no one to whom I could cry for help. From time to time I reminded myself: 'There are people out there.'

My husband came to mind, my friends, my mother, my father. This time I'd make sure I protected everyone. No one must see me, no one must look at my face. I had dirt and filth over me and I'd infect them.

In the evening we reached the city. First we went to the security building, and procedures were carried out. I got some cigarettes bought for me along the way. The prison was outside the city. On the journey it had got really dark, and you could only make out the lights.

A guard from Kirklareli security accompanied us. As we approached the prison, he said: 'It's like a five-star hotel here, very comfortable, and you'll be comfortable here.' What did it matter? Now it was a five-star hotel, now a ruin ... I didn't think about anything. My mind was completely empty. I let myself go into the future.

2

The soldier at the entrance recorded my identity. Question after question followed.

Muddling the 't' and the 'f' in the Turkish word, the soldier asked: 'Did you slander?' instead of 'Did you confess?' One of the policemen laughed and corrected the soldier before I had the chance to.

I didn't consider the question or the answer important. I was dreaming of having a bath. I didn't even look at the papers laid out for me to sign.

They were speaking among themselves: how right I was to have done this and that, how there'd be no end to this, that the state wouldn't be destroyed; they spoke to each other so that I could listen.

What did all this have to do with me? I wasn't interested any more. I was thinking only of myself, and of having a bath.

Finally it was over, and one of the policemen said: 'We sometimes have business to do here, we'll drop in on you one day.'

'OK,' I said. They left. I was free at last. I could take a deep breath.

A warder showed the way. In a room that I later learned was the lawyers' interview room a female warder searched me. For some reason I noted then that she behaved very compassionately.

'Do you want to be placed in a criminal ward or another ward?'

'I want to be on the criminal ward.'

I walked behind her. The corridor was long and dark, and the darkness intimidated me. Then we entered a big ward.

It was 6 March 1997, round about 10.30 PM. I was free of them. They didn't exist, I wouldn't see any of them again. I felt so much better, as though a ton of weight had been lifted from me. I felt myself getting lighter. My life would get back to normal.

The warder announced: 'I've brought you a new one.'

There were about two or three other people in the ward. It was a dark and murky sort of place. There was not a sound from anyone. In one corner there was an old television on a bench, two long marble tables and a few more benches; there was also a sofa there, and windows near the ceiling. At first these were what drew my attention more than the prisoners. The television seemed to be watching itself. All eyes turned towards us when the warder brought me in. There was no other reaction. Then the looks turned away again. No one was interested in a new arrival. I just stood there in the middle of the room after the warder had gone: I was on my own. No one said anything to me. I stood there stock still. No one welcomed me, no one said 'bad luck', no one showed me to a seat. I just carried on standing there like an idiot. I told myself to forget it, and sat down beside them.

'Eh, thanks for the welcome,' I said in a loud voice.

Heads turned towards me, but still there was no reaction. My God, what could I do? I was in shock. Two more women entered, making noise. They were surprised to see me and came over immediately, starting up a conversation and asking me when I'd come and why I was there. The women in the ward began to come up to me one by one. I suddenly felt I was in a scene from a film. I was among people from another world whom I didn't know or recognise. There were women between the ages of 50 and 60 and some who could only be described as children. They were all in another world, I noticed that immediately. But I wasn't in a condition to think about them.

Question followed question. Some took pity, others said: 'Forget it, it'll pass,' and when they learned that I was a political prisoner some said, 'You think you can take on the state?' and 'You're so young, it's a shame.' Everyone had their own views.

I was tired; I badly wanted a bath, and I had no clean clothes with me. I thought to myself that my mother would come the next day anyway, but I couldn't conceive of waiting until then. I had to have a bath and get myself clean as soon as possible. That was the only thought in my head.

At last someone asked me if I wanted to have a bath. I

stopped myself from screaming out, 'Yes, and as soon as possible!' and said quietly instead:

'That would be great.'

They asked if I needed help and took me to the bathroom. They brought me some clean clothes and a towel. I sent them away, saying I would manage on my own.

Finally I was in the bath, the place I'd wanted to be for days. It was as though my one aim in life were to have that bath. I was dirty, I had been dirtied, and that bath would clean me. I thought that and believed it. It had been thirteen days since I had been taken into custody. For the first time, there in the bathroom, I started really crying. The bathroom was far from the ward, and no one could have possibly heard or interrupted me. I cried, shouted, screamed and hit the walls – I couldn't do anything else. I needed no soap or shampoo. My only concern was to pour as much water as possible over my body. I remembered everything I'd lived through, but my consciousness desperately resisted accepting the reality. I felt that if I accepted it I'd be dead. Logically, I wouldn't accept it. I knew I'd go mad in that case.

I just cried and poured water over my body. That was all I could do. I was hopeless and helpless. I wanted to be a child at my mother's knee. I wanted to hug her and cry. I prayed for her to be by my side. I wouldn't have to tell her anything, just have her by me and cry on her lap. I thought of my husband too. Everything I'd lived through with him seemed to be behind a curtain of fog. There wasn't anything left to live for. The thought that he would reject me, that I would never see him again, increased the pain I was in. I was alone in the bathroom, completely alone. I don't know how long I was in there or how much I cried, but when I looked in the mirror after I came out, my face seemed to be very strange. I couldn't recognise it. It was another face in the mirror, not mine. It was swollen and red, and a pair of eyes looked out vacuously at me. My face was destroyed.

I got dressed with extraordinary difficulty. I walked, but it wasn't me who was walking. My legs were not my own ... Everything around me looked hazy and cloudy. I returned to the ward, holding onto the walls, and flopped down in a heap on the first bench I found. It was more like I had had a fresh torture session than a bath. I'd finally had my longed-for bath, but nothing had changed. My heart was constricted, and I was breathing with difficulty. I clenched my teeth. There was a rock in my chest hindering me from breathing. I thought of going to bed without anyone noticing, but I didn't know where the dormitory was, let alone an empty bed. I wanted to get to sleep so that the morning could bring a new start: a new day, a new life, a new beginning. The start of a new clean life.

The ward had two floors. The top one was the dormitory, and the bottom one was used as a mess hall. I was too exhausted to go up to the top floor. I couldn't get up from the bench for a long time. The others were looking at me strangely. They asked if I were ill. I forced myself to look normal so as to block the questions they might ask. I kept trying but I knew I was not succeeding. I was in a state where I thought I would have to answer all their questions. I didn't know what would happen if I didn't answer and I was afraid. What if they did something? I was afraid of people, afraid of myself.

But I noticed as I talked that it calmed me down, that I distanced myself from myself.

I knew the criminal wards only from watching films. I only cottoned on a little later as we talked that I had forgotten my woes and pain. Whoever I asked 'Why are you here?' the first answer was: 'Fate'. Fate had ordained this and no one was to blame!

When I went to bed late that night I felt calmer and more at ease. I kept repeating to myself: 'You'll forget.' I had to forget, to erase everything from memory. I slept well in the hope that in the morning it would all be different. My mind and body had surrendered themselves to exhaustion after thirteen days. I awoke early in the morning, feeling strong, but I was also uneasy and didn't get up for a long time. At 8: 00 AM they came to do a head count. Everyone got into a single row. No one ordered me to get up. They went off afterwards saying, 'May Allah save you.'

My first morning, my first day. I still didn't know what I'd do, and decided to go with the flow. I would start my life over from the beginning, but how and with what? All the things I had built up until then with untold effort had collapsed into rubble. First I thought of my husband. I had no power there. 'No use crying over spilt milk,' I thought, and decided one more time to let everything go. I tried to talk to people. Everyone was curious as to why I chose the criminal ward instead of the other one. I tried to shrug off the questions. I preferred to listen and answer questions with questions. In those first days, what I found most strange was how the system worked. After the head count most of the women went back to bed and got up around noon. Breakfast was at 10:00 AM, at the earliest. In time I got used to it.

Violent crime, drug dealing, adultery; there were seventeen

different crimes for seventeen separate women. Until then I had never been this close to such people. On her first visit my mother said things like, 'For God's sake, Asiye, don't fight with anyone. If you don't do anything, they won't do anything to you.' I was in shock, but theirs was even greater.

I had lived for fifteen years in the Dolapdere-Kasimpasa district of Istanbul, and spent my childhood and teenage years there. Everyone knew each other, and there was no shortage of fights and wedding celebrations. That part of the city was a world unto itself. You could find every sort in that area: Gypsies, drug dealers, people from villages, prostitutes and such like. My mother didn't often give us permission to go out on the street; we watched the fights and celebrations from our balcony. The ward at Kirklareli was rather similar. As a result I didn't find it so strange, and it wasn't difficult to get used to.

During the time I was in that prison there were two women, Sevilay and Muge, who helped me as much as they could. They both were convicted of drug offences. One was a dealer, the other a user. They never held back any material or moral support. And there was Gonul, too. She arrived one month after me.

On the third or fourth day of my imprisonment my husband's family came to visit me. We couldn't speak because we were crying so much. The day after, my mother and father came. The same scene was played out with them.

I was in Kirklareli for five months. The first days were relatively easy. They didn't make it difficult. I dedicated all my attention and energy towards forgetting my experiences at the Security HQ in Istanbul. Just to forget would make my work easier and I would be able to start my new life more easily.

The day after I arrived I was called in by the authorities, and went a little uneasily. In the director's office I met Ahmet Hashim Baran, one of those in the organisation who'd confessed. While I was kept at Security HQ he had been there too. The director said Baran wanted to talk to me, and I saw no reason not to. He asked if I needed anything, and how I was doing. I said I didn't need anything and told him I was OK. We talked for two minutes. On the way back to the ward I met Mustafa Duyar (a former fugitive and murder suspect who had confessed following his capture).

I cannot remember exactly when the problems began, cannot narrow it down. At first I tried to get to know the other prisoners. I didn't make any plans for the future – I wasn't in a position to do so anyway. I was helped in my efforts to forget what I had been through by constantly talking to people. I was interested in their lives and tried to get them to tell me their experiences; or I watched television. Sometimes I sat watching television for hours without noticing the time as it went by.

The women in the ward generally remarked that I was lost in thought. About a month later my sleep started becoming disturbed. I would wake up sweating from nightmares. I didn't tell anyone anything. One of the women in the neighbouring bunk remarked after a while that I groaned a lot at night. I wasn't conscious of this. My efforts to get back to sleep after the nightmares were in vain. I was desperate. I tried to forget, but everything returned obstinately to my head. The thought didn't occur to me of talking or telling my story, and even if it had come to my mind, to whom would I tell it? I was running even from myself.

One night I again woke up screaming, but couldn't come to.

A man was chasing me, and I heard a constant, terrible laughter. The others tried for a long time to awaken me, without success. Finally Emine started reading the Kur'ân and praying by my bed. The last resort!

Emine was one of my best friends in Kirklareli. She was very old and a refugee from Bulgaria who had lived there since childhood and been a member of the Komsomol, the Communist Youth Party of the Soviets. She came to Turkey at the beginning of the 1990s, and had been convicted of murdering her husband.

The things that I had been trying to erase from my memory came back in fragments. The days when I thought I was well and at ease started receding. I couldn't allow this – I'd go mad! There was no other way out than to forget. On top of that, my period was late. What if I was pregnant? Just thinking of that took my breath away. I had to go to the doctor and find out, trying to remain cool and calm.

Tthe sick-bay the doctor behaved as though he wanted to get the whole thing over with as soon as possible.

'I want to have a pregnancy test,' I said.

'How long have you been in prison?'

'About a month.'

The doctor gave me a strange look, which I didn't understand at first.

'No, I don't mean that. I'm asking what prison you came from.'

'I came from the Security HQ.'

'Oh, that's different. I thought you'd been in prison for a long time.'

I realised why he had asked that question. A woman in the

ward for those who had confessed had recently given birth. She had been in prison a long time. I realised the doctor was familiar with such events.

A few days later I got the referral and went to the hospital. How did those hours and days pass? Every minute, every second was a different nightmare. I didn't speak with anyone; I stayed in my bunk and didn't come down to eat. Nor did I sleep. I had violent bouts of crying, when I wanted to smash and break everything. I had a plan of action. From everywhere I gathered up painkillers. If I had turned out to be pregnant I would have taken them all at once. I had always wanted to be a mother; my husband and I had often dreamed about it, but our options had not allowed it then. To want to be a mother and then after torture give birth to a child by a police torturer! The very thought was too hard to put into words. I didn't know how I would manage, but it was a feeling like death.

When I got the result of the test I thought I'd die of joy. It came out negative. Upon my return from the hospital I embraced the first person I came across in the ward. There were women who knew why I had gone to the hospital. They thought, of course, that I might have been pregnant by my husband. When told the result of the test was negative, they were sad on my behalf. They couldn't have understood my joy. How could they? Most of them gave me strange looks.

One month after I'd arrived, the ward had its first release. One woman's three-year sentence for violent crime had finished. The night before her release we had great fun in the ward. Everyone was happy. Those worried faces, those eyes always ready to cry, could laugh for at least a short time. I couldn't join in the dancing but I was content just to watch. (I, who had only reluctantly danced at my own wedding, was not about to get up then to dance and show off.) Thoughtfully, they didn't insist too much. Despite the suffering and longing, they didn't miss this opportunity to turn the ward into a celebration.

Those were the days when the 'amnesty bill' was on the agenda. A few people in the ward followed the news very carefully. If the word 'amnesty' was mentioned the atmosphere in the ward changed in a moment. We watched the nightly news on television. The Council of Ministers broadcast an announcement – something like, 'the state is merciful, showing how generous it is'. When this was heard, applause broke out immediately. 'There's going to be an amnesty, we'll be saved,' the prisoners began to shout. Some prayed to God, others cried with joy. Those who had been asleep jumped out of their beds. Hearing the noise, the warders came running. The shouting turned to songs. There was no need for tapes or radio – they made the music themselves, sang themselves, danced themselves. Some of them left the dancing from time to time and asked me questions since I was a politico. What could I say? If I'd said then: 'It's not possible, there won't be an amnesty,' I would have been viewed as the worst person in the world. Everyone had hope in their hearts, and most of them would succeed in holding onto this hope in prison. Either I didn't give an opinion or got out of it by saying I didn't know. Some of the women remarked: 'You don't know anything either; what sort of a politico are you?'

There were some among the prisoners who knew revolutionaries. Though most of them were in prison on charges of drugs or violence, they knew revolutionaries because they had been incarcerated at Bayrampasa prison at various times. Sevilay had given birth to her son, now three or four years old, in Bayrampasa; he was named Ali Haydar after a famous revolutionary figure from the 1970s.

My family and my husband's family frequently visited me. They did not leave me on my own. At the end of April, my husband's sisters brought me a notebook so that I could write in it. What would I write, what would I tell? I wondered. One week later I started writing in it, more to pass the time than anything else. I was putting down on paper the life of the ward, or what I did all day. That was all. I didn't, couldn't, touch upon anything else.

Later, a relative who was a lawyer came to see me. We hadn't seen each other for a long time, and I had but a few childhood memories of him. His family had lived on the floor above us, and he had been very naughty as a child. My grandmother sometimes used to come from her village to Istanbul to stay with us. When she went back to the village she used to warn those in the house sternly: 'Don't let my girl Asiye be beaten up by Haluk.' Later his family moved, and so did mine. During my university years I saw him a couple of times.

At first I felt strange. Ghosts from my childhood passed through my mind. We talked about home and relatives, gossiping about the family and never getting to the real heart of the matter. 'So we've got a person who confessed in the family,' he finally said. I didn't tell him that I hadn't confessed. He asked what I would do at court and I said I didn't want to appear there.

He emphasised that I had to leave Kirklareli. He reminded me that I shouldn't turn my face away from human values.

No, I didn't think leaving the prison was best. How could I look people in the face? I definitely would not put in a request for transfer. I didn't want to talk any longer; these thoughts and these feelings were coursing through my bloodstream.

But I said to Haluk: 'OK, I'll put in the request.'

When he went, he left me a form for the request. Later I tore up the sheet of paper and threw it in the bin. I would start a new life here. No one was going to make me put in a request for a transfer. I had to forget the past, and I wouldn't forget it if I went to another place.

I was in a constant state of panic, but I tried to keep calm. At first I took a bath twice or even three or four times a day. I thought that would remove the dirt on me. There were scars, and I had to erase those scars to leave nothing of the past. This wasn't a physical impression, it was just a feeling – as though people would look at my face and recognise it. It was enough to horrify me. So I rushed to take a bath, but felt worse after each and every one. There was only one thing to do – to cry. At such times I was dumbfounded and desperate for an outlet. I felt I'd explode from the distress inside me and I tried to chase away the worries in my head and occupy myself with other things. But it were as though I would explode at any moment. I kept urging myself to be calm and let it pass. I found things I could do with my hands. In the ward they made ornaments from wood and beads, and I tried to learn how to make them. I made gifts for everyone, and soon started making lace, too. When I was a child my mother tried to get my sisters and me to make lace. My father came out against this, saying, 'My daughters should go to school!' Before long I had made a small table- and coffee-table-coverings and lace fringes on towels. I learned how to do beadwork and wickerwork as well.

Thus I succeeded in filling time. If I wasn't able to do anything I watched television or wrote home to my sister. I tried not to stay on my own. I still wasn't sleeping at night, and kept having nightmares. I was afraid to sleep. I couldn't escape from the dreams or their after-effects, and it took me a very long while to regain my senses at such times. As a result I gave up the struggle to sleep. At 2:00 AM the mess hall closed, so I sat there up until then, kept company by other prisoners who hung about there as well. I could stay up as long as I wanted in the dormitory after that because the lights weren't put out; I only tried to get to sleep when the day was dawning. I slept better during the day.

One and a half or two months after my arrival I was told that the prison governor wanted to see me, and I went to him.

'You have a visitor from Istanbul.'

'From Istanbul?'

'From Security.'

I had to keep cool, keep calm, look normal.

'OK.'

I was taken to a room full of people. I saw Ahmet Hashim Baran. There was someone sitting in a corner whom I recognised from the Security HQ. Mustafa Duyar, who had also been there, sat in another corner, talking amongst a group of people. There were others I did not recognise. My head spun, and I had to force myself not to fall. I wanted to run away.

'How are you, Asiye?' they asked.

'I'm well.'

'What will you do in court? Will you take back your statement?'

'I won't go to court.'

'Have you had any news from your husband?'

'No.'

'Girl, you should divorce that man. Surely any man would contact his wife?'

I made no reply to this.

'Has any lawyer come to see you?'

'My relative who is a lawyer came.'

'We know that. Has any other lawyer come?'

'No.'

This was turning into a second interrogation. I couldn't stay there any longer. I said I had something to do and returned to the ward.

Towards evening a packet of cigarettes appeared and with it some perfume and a box of shampoo. I gave them out to anyone who needed them.

I felt myself forced into a corner. I had worked so hard to forget what had happened, and now this latest incident had brought it all back. I embraced sleep again – if I could sleep, time would pass more easily.

Some days later Semra Polat came back to the ward. She had been with us for a while, then left, but now she had returned. We had a series of brief conversations. She spoke about Bayrampasa, but had a strange air about her. She frightened me and I tried to keep away from her. Soon afterwards the daily life of the ward became more tense. Semra began to fight with everyone; she picked arguments for the flimsiest of reasons.

At the beginning of May new prisoners were transferred to the ward – two women expelled from Bakirkoy prison in Istanbul following a revolt there, and one from Afyon, a Romanian by birth. The ward was now very crowded. Some women were scheduled for transfer to other prisons.

There was an old 'auntie' among those who were going to Sivas. She had murdered her husband and dismembered him with an axe, and was very badly off. She was the woman I most wanted to get to know, but I was never able to grab the opportunity to do so. Unless I was mistaken, she had no one apart from a daughter and a son, and sent them money that she tried to save from doing various handiwork – she had secured a living by doing cleaning, ironing and washing for some other prisoners when she was in Bayrampasa. She used to describe what she'd done in a very cold- blooded manner, as though she felt no remorse. Before she went to sleep she always had to read the bits of newspapers she picked up here and there. She used to say she couldn't go to sleep if she hadn't read them.

There was another one among those going to Sivas who had got a life sentence for murdering her niece. Murder after the torture of a little child! I tried to keep my distance from this woman. She claimed she had been forced to confess and that she hadn't committed the crime. The general consensus of the ward was on the side of her having done it. The criminal wards had their own law. Those who came in for certain crimes were not to be trusted. When she was in Bayrampasa, this woman had been frequently beaten by the other prisoners. From time to time some small things went missing, but no one suspected the prisoners convicted for theft. 'A thief robs on the outside, but not here.'

My friend Gonul was among those who came from Bakirkoy, a frank girl who spoke her mind. She was in for armed violence, if I remember correctly, and loved revolutionaries. Soon after I arrived we developed a warm friendship, and started preparing our food together. Gonul had come to prison at the age of seventeen or eighteen, and been inside for almost five years. She had run away from her family when her father began demanding money. Her mother's only woe was that living in Kayseri, she had gone into Kayseri prison. Gonul went on a hunger strike to the death with one other prisoner from the ward in 1996; I can't remember how long she endured, but she lasted a long time.

Haluk came a second time. This time Gulizar Hanim came with him. She had been my lawyer when I was working on the newspaper.

'You need to take an honest stand to get on your feet,' Gulizar said. She asked some questions relating to rape. How could she do that, I thought! It was impossible, I just didn't want to hear about it. No one apart from me could know what had happened.

'There was nothing like that,' I said. 'I don't want to talk about that.'

They kept insisting that I should leave the prison. I insisted that I should stay on and that I wouldn't be able to look anyone in the face.

'If you stay here it'll get worse. All your life you'll never look anyone in the face.'

'Fine,' I said. 'But if I stay here I won't run the risk of seeing anyone.'

'How is it, looking at your face?'

'I look now how I look.'

The conversation went on, but finally I agreed to request a transfer.

You need to take an honest stand to get on your feet. These words lodged themselves in my mind. What did it mean? Why should I get on my feet? If I got on my feet, what would change? What would I gain? I'd lost everything! What did I have left? If I got on my feet would what I had lost come back? I would just have more pain, that's all. I was trying to make a new life for myself, so I'd start anew. If I tried to get on my feet, that wouldn't happen. I wasn't going to build my life on ruins – it would only collapse again. There were ruins all around; I'd jumped over them and passed on, and I was starting again. Nothing outside me interested me. I was starting life again!

A few days after this conversation I was eating with Gonul. During a pause, she asked me: 'Did you confess?'

My mouthful stuck in my throat. It was as if a huge, random piece of rock had smashed into me, as though someone had violently pushed me, as though for the second time I was rolling down into an abyss.

'No,' I said, so softly I could hardly hear myself.

'Then why are you here?'

I couldn't give an answer.

That day it was as though Gonul had violently slapped me. Her question 'Did you confess?' shook up every cell in my body. It roughed me up, burned my soul.

After that question everything started getting more difficult. I kept asking myself: 'Did I confess?' My answer was no, but I couldn't explain why I was here. I had to remain distant from the thought, because if I couldn't give an answer that meant I couldn't face myself.

I didn't want this. I was escaping from myself. I didn't want to remember, I wanted a 'normal' life, far from everything and everyone.

You need to take an honest stand to get on your feet.

Did you confess?

Now I was coming and going between these two sentences, and they wouldn't leave my mind. It was as though my helplessness were steadily growing. I tried not to be around Gonul, but her question played constantly on my mind and, like it or not, I had to provide some answers to myself.

Soon I found a handwritten note on my bed. 'We know everything,' it read. 'You can't fool us. Either get the hell out of here or else ... '

It was clear from whom the note had come: Semra Polat. Everything was coming in on top of each other. One day Semra, who had confessed, fought with Gonul and got a good beating. No one came between them: the other women did not move so much as a finger. Then finally one of them said, 'That's enough, now she's seeing sense,' and went to separate them, followed by the others. Not a long time passed before she began fighting again, with Muge this time. The warders took action this time, and Semra Polat was put in a small cell opposite the booths used for meetings. Words I had instigated against her started circulating openly in the ward, but I didn't expend any energy on them. Questions burrowed into my brain, wouldn't leave my mind – I was divided in two.

Inside me a second 'I' was growing again. One half of me wanted to go, and the other resisted and said no. How would I

face people, how would I look them in the face? I had no
strength for that. I was not a person who confessed, and I did
not want to be labelled one. But I didn't want to go back again.

Gonul would not let me be: 'If you haven't confessed, why
are you staying here?' she would ask. 'If I were in your place I
wouldn't stay one second.' If she didn't say this in words, she
said it with her eyes.

Time passed. My nerves were taut, and I had to make a
decision. I was afraid. How would I go and what would I do
when I'd gone? My sleep grew more disturbed. On the one
hand there were the constant nightmares, and on the other, the
question of going or not was continuously revolving in my
mind. Everything was mixed up. Despite the fact that Semra
Polat was away from the ward, I had no peace. Gonul, Sevilay
and Muge formed a circle around me. The focus of the
problem was to go or not to go, to accept that I'd confessed or
to reject the false circumstances of my 'confession'. What
would this mean? If I stayed in that prison, willingly or
unwillingly, I would stay as one who'd confessed. I had no
other option. If I left, what would I say to people? I didn't even
begin to consider returning to my old life or not. OK, so I'd see
no one and stay in the independent ward. One court hearing
would be enough.

Then my life would return to normal.

What sort of normal? Is it normal now?

I wanted to live honourably and morally. I wasn't the only
one who had been defeated by the torturers.

*But you've been raped. You're not clean any more, you can't
look people in the face. You can't talk, laugh with them, eat
with them.*

'But they don't know about it.'

It's enough that you know.

'It's not like that.'

You may think not, but you are proud, you won't be able to look people in the eye. You came here and you can't go back.

I was proud, wasn't I? And I'd become two people again. One side said 'go', the other side cursed it all and said 'stay'.

The court date was fixed: 4 June. I was thinking about whether or not to go. If I did go I'd meet a whole lot of people there. How would I look at their faces? How would I say hello to them? If I was put in another prison I wouldn't be able to hold my head up. My nerves had never been more raw. I couldn't eat any food. If I did eat anything my stomach started turning and I vomited; my weight fell to 45 kilos. I tried not to be on my own. If I were alone I started talking to myself and I didn't want that, so I made an effort to occupy myself or stayed near people. I was running away from myself. I avoided Gonul's looks and hid in every nook and cranny, frightened to death. I would eat myself up with worry. I was completely overwhelmed.

One morning it was as though I'd really woken up and I put in the request for transfer.

'I want to go to a prison near my family,' I said.

How I did this, how I found the strength to do it, I don't know. Everything happened in a flash. Damn it, I told myself. Have I got any pride, any honour left? Come what may, let's get it over with; I can't go on running away, fearful as an insect of its own shadow. Let's get it over with.

I was afraid, but what would happen if the police sensed that? I might be taken to the Security HQ. No, that was impossible! I phoned Haluk, who said he would come in a couple of days, along with my father. I'd tell him of my intention. I'd say that I needed help, that I didn't want to stay here. Haluk would speak with the authorities. My father would also put in a request.

I didn't go to court on the appointed day – anyway, I hadn't been summoned. Within a month my request for transfer was refused. I put in another request immediately, and my father put in another as well. They went to Ankara to speed up the process. But I received the same answer.

Now I was desperate and on the point of giving up, but I made a third attempt.

'I fear for my life in this prison,' I insisted in the request.

The waiting was terrible. I kept reminding myself to keep calm. I tried to sleep, but my sleep was still very disturbed; I chose a few books from the library list, and read two by Peyami Safa. Gonul had *Like Ivy on the Wall* and some other books, which I read. There was another book, a collection of poems by Hasan Huseyin which I couldn't put down. I continued to make lace. I made little trinkets from wicker. I tried to fill my time. The weather got better and we started playing ball. I tried to wake up early a few times to do sport but I couldn't continue. My constitution had become very weak, and I tired very quickly. Sometimes I had to force myself to stay on my feet – if I lay down I'd be left with myself and that was the last thing I wanted.

Muge stayed up late at nights, so I sat with her. She had been involved with drugs, and had been in prison for a total of ten years at different times in her life. She smoked almost three packs of cigarettes a day. Muge had left a cold impression on me when I first saw her, but when I got to know her I soon loved her. Sometimes she held nothing back when trying to make me cross, but I couldn't be cross with her. She used to say things that would have sparked me off had they come from someone else, yet I wasn't able to be angry with her. She had a young son. I never saw him, as he was never brought to the prison. In any event he knew her as his auntie, not his mother. Since she was involved with drugs, she wanted it that way. Muge shocked me with the richness of her world. There seemed to be nothing she hadn't experienced. She used to recount episodes from her life to me, like how she'd been in hospital to come off heroin but had been able to find drugs even more easily there. She told stories about gambling until dawn, and about her experiences at every Security HQ whenever she'd been arrested. But she had a way of telling these things as though her life had been not painful but happy.

What shocked me most was that she had started taking drugs after getting married – which drove her husband to suicide. I couldn't determine to what extent this had affected Muge. Every so often she'd start off: 'Eh, Asiye. In the old days it didn't affect us at all – I went in like a lioness and came out equally strong. I don't know whether I've just grown old, but I can't take it – I came in like a lioness but I'll come out like a mouse.' She also read coffee grounds. When she was asked to wash up she used to say: 'Come on, you do the washing up and I'll tell your fortune.' As a result of these readings we seized the opportunity to drink lots of coffee.

After I had put in my transfer request she used to say at every fortune-telling session: 'I see you are going on a long journey. You are really going to go.'

Thanks to Muge I started laughing again. Some nights we got stomach cramps from laughing so hard. The things that made us laugh were painful; we laughed at the pain.

Finally the governor called me in – I had feared this. I went expecting that they had come again from the Security HQ. But this time I didn't recognise those who came, though I surmised that they had heard about my wish to transfer.

However, they didn't ask direct questions. They asked whether or not I was thinking of leaving, and whether or not, if I were to leave, I would rescind my statement.

I said that I was thinking of not going, and that if I were to go I would stay in the independent ward and wouldn't take back my statement. They had no intention of talking for a long time. They asked about my husband again. As I was going back I went into the governor's room. I told him I didn't want talk to anyone from Security HQ.

The governor said, 'No one's going to force you to see them against your will.'

Haluk continued to come often. As each day went by I became more and more devoid of hope. I would have changed my mind, but I was hopeful that my last request would succeed. I decided I would go on hunger strike if I didn't get an answer three weeks after I lodged the request.

Again, I don't know where I got the strength, but I began my hunger strike on 31 June. Gonul joined me. Her aim was to be transferred to Kayseri prison. She couldn't make a transfer request before one year was up, as she was 'exiled'; her requests had all been turned down.

At this time Muge and Sevilay were experiencing difficulties with the authorities as a result of Semra Polat. Her version to them of what went on in the ward was put in a very different light. Then Semra married Mustafa Duyar. A wedding dress was brought in and she wandered around the ward in it for the whole day.

On the sixth day of the hunger strike, on the pretext that the governor wanted to see them, Sevilay, Muge and Gonul were taken out of the ward and sent to other prisons. As far as I could gather from the letters that followed, they were all sent to different prisons. I was alone and in shock as though my circle of protection had suddenly disappeared. I felt like a fish out of water. I panicked – I didn't know what to do. My head was thoroughly muddled. The same day I got a positive response to my request for transfer. I ceased my hunger strike. I didn't know whether to be happy or sad. Was it the right thing to do? I was so confused. I had no choice but to believe. Two more days had not fully elapsed before I got the news that as Gebze prison was full, my transfer had been cancelled. I resumed the hunger strike.

Half the ward was really sympathetic to me. Apart from a couple of women, no one advised me to stop striking. Moreover, they encouraged me to go on with it to the end. This, too, gave me strength.

There was a woman there named Tombul. She had been sentenced to over 100 years for committing murder and violence. She also began a hunger strike as a protest against her sentence. She continued for almost 50 days, then was talked out of it and abandoned the strike.

I didn't know how long my hunger strike would go on for. I had never gone on a long one. Tombul was experienced: she brought me lemonade with sugar three times a day. She also tried to make me drink water often. The doctor was contacted, and despite the fact that I felt quite well they tried to get him to see me. No one ate food in my presence; I was shocked at how sensitively they were behaving.

Tombul said: 'On the day you break your hunger strike I'll make you pasta with yoghurt and garlic.' She loved this dish, and often made it – I had been frequently invited to join her.

On 28 July I was told again that my transfer had come through. I said I wouldn't give up the hunger strike until I had laid eyes on the official document, and they showed me the letter from the Ministry.

'For the sake of the prisoner's security, she should be transferred to Gebze prison immediately … ' I read it again and again. I looked at the signatures and seals; I took down the reference numbers.

They said I would be on my way within a couple of days, so I gave up the hunger strike. That evening Tombul lived up to her promise. I ate pasta with lots of yoghurt and garlic – my stomach was fine. Later I wondered whether I should have waited to come off the strike until I was on my way.

I didn't know whether or not I was happy. I didn't know what I felt. After I had put in my first request, my only aim was to leave Kirklareli whatever happened. I hadn't thought about what I would come up against, what I would say and do. Now it was time for these things.

Around that time I received a typewritten letter in the post from Istanbul; my husband's name was on the envelope. Although I knew he would never do this, the letter still upset me. It said that he wanted me to start divorce proceedings, and was full of strange statements. It was not possible at such a

time for me not to be affected: however much I believed that I
had lost him, he was still one of my strongholds. When I read
the letter I couldn't cry, despite the fact that not a day had
passed in the last five months without my crying. I was frozen.
It was as though I had been hit by a bullet. Our life together
passed in front of my eyes. I started blaming him as though he
were guilty of what I had had to live through – now he was
pulling out halfway down the road.

Why are you upset? It was obvious this would happen.

'*How could he do this. He was my everything.*'

But you finished it.

'*Alright, but he shouldn't have done this.*'

*You were starting a new life and he has no place in that life.
You're on your own now. Whatever you do you'll do alone,
relying on yourself.*

'*No, he shouldn't have done this now. He shouldn't have
pulled out halfway. He should have supported and helped me.
He should have tried to understand.*'

But what if the letter were not from him? I had not been in
a position until then to think much about my husband. I
believed that I had lost him when I was raped at the Security
HQ. I tried to go on as though he didn't exist. Judging by how
much that letter affected me, I wasn't very successful at all. I
got a warder to phone my husband's uncle and asked him to
come. I had to be sure whether the letter had come from my
husband or from someone else.

A couple of days later my visitor came and I told him of the
letter. He said my husband had done nothing of the sort and
was angry with me, asking how I could have believed that. I
couldn't hold my tears back any longer and cried.

On the same day they said, 'Get ready, you'll be setting off soon.' The warder's voice rang in my ears.

I didn't have many things to get together. I was ready.

We set off at two o'clock in the afternoon of 31 July. There were three people apart from me in the prison van. Two were criminals going to Bayrampasa for treatment. One person involved in the PKK (Kurdistan Workers' Party) case was going with me to Gebze. As I got into the prison van I felt very out of sorts. I was afraid I might be taken to another place – I just couldn't be sure.

My hands were bound with chains. I wanted to look back before I got in but I couldn't, as I had to get into the van so fast.

Then we set off for Gebze.

The weather was very hot. Inside the van it was like hell, no breeze at all. It was a long journey.

I was in a half-faint all the way. I felt exhausted and weak because the weather was hot and because I had only recently abandoned my hunger strike. I felt a strange light-headedness; I was afraid something would go wrong, but at the same time I felt calm and untroubled. I didn't know how I would be received. When I was saying farewell to the women in the ward at Kirklareli, the old auntie said through tears: 'Look girl, let's not be getting any bad news from there.' These words came into my mind but I didn't dwell on them.

When everything in your life loses meaning for you, what is left that is more valuable than death? It was all I had.

I wasn't completely sure why and how I had decided to leave Kirklareli. What pushed me to leave there was the same thing that drew me to Gebze. But I wasn't sure whether I wanted it or not. It was life and the wish to live that took me there. When

I thought I had lost everything I didn't stop to think what this would mean in my life. The wish to live pressed down on me. Despite all manner of suffering, human beings don't easily give up on life. This counted for me too. The only thing I hadn't given up was breathing; otherwise I had no plans to give meaning to life. I didn't ask if one could live like this. Some did. Why couldn't I?

3

I wanted to look at the Bosphorus, but I was in no state to stand up. I wanted to struggle onto my feet and see outside. The air had grown quite cool at this late evening hour, but the van's windows were very small and it was dark outside, so I could only make out the lights with difficulty. I couldn't figure out where we had gone and where we were.

Around 10:00 PM we reached Gebze. The van stopped in the prison garden. We waited for about ten minutes without being told to get out – I really hated the waiting. I heard voices arguing outside but I couldn't make out what their words. A soldier was saying there was a problem.

Fear overwhelmed me – I'd come this far, and I wouldn't return! Then the vehicle door was open; the garden stretched out like a green carpet.

At last an officer said, 'Come out.' I went through the door. I was afraid my legs wouldn't carry me. For a time I stumbled and swayed. My things remained in the prison van. It was unbelievable, I could hardly stand, I had to find somewhere to sit. As we entered I saw that there were a lot of people in that place, but I couldn't see any familiar faces.

Finally a warder pointed me to a chair.

'Sit down, sister.'

I could barely throw myself onto the chair. My hands were still bound with chains.

'Haven't you got any things?'

Feebly, I said, 'Yes', but didn't have the strength to take it any further. Then they took off the chains. I needed to win some time to think, so I closed my eyes. I didn't know what I'd do. I needed to call someone to me, but I couldn't manage it. New people kept coming in.

I was able to make out a face I knew. It was a friend with whom I'd worked on the newspaper for some time, who hadn't changed. I lost feeling in my limbs, but got to my feet with difficulty.

She held out her hand and said, 'Welcome.' I took her hand and wanted to hold it firmly, but I had no strength – I was ashamed and couldn't look her in the face.

'Thanks,' I said. I don't know whether or not she could hear my voice. I couldn't think of anything – I was excited, afraid, ashamed. I wanted the earth to open and swallow me up. I didn't know how I'd behave. I experienced dozens of feelings in one moment.

'Let's go to the ward.' We came to the ward door.

'Oh, my boss has come,' I heard a voice say.

I recognised the voice but wasn't able to turn round. The shame I felt was terrible; I also had difficulty breathing, as though a hand were clutching my throat. I wanted to embrace the owner of the voice, but there were so many things getting in my way and holding on to me. Yet I was shocked at how calm I was; I couldn't understand how I could be so calm.

'You've got very thin ,'said the familiar voice.

'I've been on hunger strike, that's why.'

'When did you come off it?'

'The day before yesterday.'

'How are you?'

'Fine.'

Actually I wasn't feeling fine at all. My knees were about to buckle and I had to lean against the wall. The words were stuck in my throat. We were in front of the women's ward. Then I saw two faces I knew – we had been taken into custody at the same time.

I embraced everyone, or rather they embraced me. I didn't want to cry but I couldn't hold back my tears. I started to cry, though I didn't know why. The faces I'd thought I'd never see again, the embraces, holding of hands, the welcoming words, the laughter, people asking how I was, the shame I felt, the pain and joy, all mingled together. But it was shame that I felt the strongest. If only I had died, and not seen these people in this way.

We entered the ward. I felt a flush of fever – I was sweating. The first thing I saw was flowers. There had been no flowers in Kirklareli; here there were violets in abundance.

They showed me to a seat and prepared something for me to eat. People said, 'Welcome.' I was on the verge of panic again. I was in shock – I couldn't look people in the face or eyes. I gave answers, but did they hear me? I had difficulty hearing my voice.

Someone I didn't know sat beside me. She assumed I had come from Bayrampasa and was asking after her friends there. I hung my head. I couldn't say, 'I've come from Kirklareli.' I just couldn't. Then someone replied for me: 'She's come from Kirklareli.'

My God, why had I come here? If only I hadn't come, at least I wouldn't have had to face these sorts of questions. I had been OK, but this was different, how could I look at people? But I told myself that I must keep calm.

'You probably want a bath.'

'Of course I do.'

I had a bath and became calmer. But I was dead tired. I wanted to go to sleep immediately. There was no spare bed, so I had to sleep with a friend. I wanted to fall asleep at once, but despite my exhaustion I couldn't get to sleep.

I closed my eyes and tried to think, although I was not in any condition to do so. All my feelings had been turned upside down. When I awoke in the morning, for the first time in months I noticed that I had slept well: an impenetrable, dreamless, nightmare-less sleep. This was the first morning in Gebze. It was Friday.

I remember all the details connected with this day. People were trying to speak to me but I didn't have anything to say. I couldn't look at anyone directly because I felt so ashamed. It was as though the fact that I had come from Kirklareli were branded on my forehead. It was as though everyone was looking, staring at me as though I were an inferior form of life.

I felt like that, so I believed it.

I had wanted to come to Gebze and had come here at last, and after the first evening I no longer said, 'If only I hadn't come here.' But I did say, and often: 'If only I had managed to die.'

I couldn't think at all. I didn't know what to do, and I didn't want to know. I didn't want anyone to talk to me, to struggle with me – I just wanted to be left in peace, nothing else. I would go to the court and announce that I had been forced to sign the statements under torture. I couldn't say anything else. Let no one ask or request anything else. Let them leave me to live how I wanted. I'd have no complaints.

I didn't want to come down off my bunk or to go out to the exercise yard. I didn't want anyone to see me.

That day it felt as though the evening would never come, as if time had stopped and wasn't going forward. I kept thinking that if evening could come quickly, I could go to bed, still with no one seeing me.

My first days at Gebze went by with great difficulty. People – my dear friends – clung to me and wanted to talk. What could I tell them? That I had been raped? I would never dream of it. No strength could make me tell that.

An incident happened about a week after I arrived at Gebze. One of our friends, who was pregnant when arrested, gave birth. A tiny little pink-red creature came into the ward. For some days I was only able to look at the baby from a distance; I wasn't brave enough to come close. It was as though I thought I would dirty the baby if I came too close, loved it, looked at it. It was absolutely clean, a sparkling new life. To come close, to touch it would remind me of life. I was sure of this and that's why I tried to keep my distance. Life was very far away from me. Also, I was jealous of the mother. I had no chance any more of becoming a mother, despite the fact that I had yearned for it so much once.

But a tornado-like wind was pushing me to it. I thought I'd die of fear when I first took the baby into my arms. What if it cried or if it wouldn't want to stay in my arms? But it wasn't aware of anything; it was so distant from the dirt and horrors of the world. How would it grasp that I was dirtied? I didn't hold the baby in my arms for long. I gave it back to its mother and went and cried in the toilet.

It was the morning of my second or third day. I was going down to breakfast and met a little girl on the stairs; I hadn't yet met her mother and didn't even know her name. I was going down and she was coming up. She stopped right in front of me and said:

'How are you?'

'I'm well.'

'Can I kiss you?'

I leaned over and she kissed my cheek. I was shocked. I couldn't understand it; she didn't even know me. Why would she do this? At that moment I thought, what a strange child.

As she left, she said, 'Please be well, sister.'

Nothing held any interest for me any longer. Everything was distant. I tried to read to pass the time, but did so very slowly. Either I didn't understand what I was reading, or I didn't notice that I had phased out and then woken up and returned to the book. I did only what I could do unconsciously: eat, read the paper and sleep. Sleep was my escape from my surroundings and from myself.

My friends had decided to latch onto me. I was fed up, distressed, unable to breathe properly.

My absent-mindedness increased enormously. If no one spoke to me, I didn't make an effort to speak to anyone. When I did talk it always seemed to me that I was coming from another world. I was frightened by everything, by everyone. If someone spoke loudly beside me I became frightened; if someone passed by me as I was washing my hands in the basin I became afraid; and I was startled by every little touch to get my attention.

The person who tried most to talk to me was my friend from the newspaper. She tried to work out why I had gone to Kirklareli, why I had signed false statements. One evening I was talking to Arif, another former colleague – or rather, he was talking to me. (Men and women could meet regularly in the lawyers' room on the women's ward.) He was making an effort to get me to share and express my thoughts. I gave short answers to the usual questions. I didn't look at his face. I hung my head and looked at the floor. I knew he was trying to help but I was too ashamed to want his help. But part of me did want it, because I realised I'd rot away or go mad if I continued as I was. I didn't want it, because to want it and to face it meant to accept reality. That meant more pain and agony, whereas I wanted to forget everything and bury myself deeply and live an ordinary life.

I didn't want to talk about my having been raped. I would hide it and not talk about it. If I did talk about it, what would people think? What would my parents say if they heard? These things were eating into my brain.

People spoke of facing up to things, facing up to oneself. It

was just this that I ran away from, hiding however I could. I
couldn't bear the idea of 'facing up'; it would increase my pain
a thousandfold, a millionfold. I was so weak I couldn't endure
it; I wanted to live, but just to breathe. If I faced up to it, I
would die.

'They raped me,' I said in desperation.

I didn't know what made me say it. I was crying; the abyss
could have swallowed me up.

'Look at my face, look into my eyes,' Arif said. 'All our
hatred is against those who did this. Why are you ashamed? It's
those bastards who should be ashamed. Hold your head up
high.'

I'd said it. I'd told someone, but on the condition that he
promise not to tell anyone else. He said that it was wrong to
keep it a secret, that I should reveal it and call the perpetrators
to account, but that if I didn't want to, he wouldn't tell anyone
either.

I returned to the ward in tears. How could I have told when
I wasn't going to? A voice within me had commanded it: *Tell!*

The second 'I' that I had discovered within me over the
previous months spoke to me again. This time it was on my
side. *Tell*, it insisted. *You'll go through more pain but you'll
wake up feeling better in the morning.* But I neither slept better
nor woke up feeling better.

Only one person knew: but it was out. I was eaten up inside.
What would people think of me, how would they look at me?

The second 'I' inside me had taken over and begun to speak.
It had tried to make me say things I didn't want to say and do
things I didn't want to do. I had had absolutely no intention of
telling about the rape. It was to have remained my secret.

That second 'I' always emerged at the most difficult moments. It wasn't there when I wanted it, and it spoke to me when I didn't want it to.

I had to find something to hold on to. My knees were trembling. I couldn't stand. What or whom could I hold on to? My husband? Never ... I was trying to get him out of my mind. He wouldn't accept me in this state. My mother and father? No, they wouldn't understand me ... My brothers and sisters? No, they'd say, 'You're to blame.' A green branch? It would wither. The sky? If I looked at it, it would turn grey. I stretched out my hand and everywhere pushed me back. I pulled back my hand the moment I drew close. I was ashamed, ashamed to death. The things that came into my head were all to do with death, all my plans were for death.

My plans – yes, I began to make plans – were for dying, not for living. I avoided everything that reminded me of life. Every day I drew closer to the end. This was my escape.

What held me? How can I tell you? On the one hand I was running fast towards death, and on the other, I felt I was putting distance between it and me. I backed away from it when I spoke with people and approached it when I was alone. The baby that came to the ward, the little girl who kissed me; friends and soulmates coming close: these were my support. But most important was my turning to support myself. Soon I began to ensure that I didn't stay on my own. I wanted to be with someone all the time, so they would talk with me, not leave me alone – for I'd die if I were alone. I was afraid I would die, flailing like a reptile on the ground. When I went to bed at night I tried to go to sleep, not thinking about a thing. If I didn't go to sleep thousands of questions would attack my mind.

Hope, that infernal possibility, had attached itself to me. I was changing every day, hour by hour, minute by minute. Sometimes I wanted to disappear from everyone's sight. For hours on end I didn't speak, but sometimes I could talk incessantly, without pausing for breath. At such times I used to say to myself: 'Is this me who's talking?' Those who'd known me before were shocked. Basically, these moments were just a form of escape, when I avoided the things that tormented me. I was also running away from questions that sought my answers. However much I talked, however much I created a dialogue with people, I still remained distant from myself.

At first my sleep was comparatively good. From time to time I had nightmares, though not that often anymore. I kept everything down. I expended a terrific amount of energy to prevent things from coming to the surface.

Those first days I had difficulty getting used to the regime there. There was no comparison with the ordered days of my life at Kirklareli. The schedule for going to bed and getting up and the times for eating were different every day.

My friends did everything in their power to make me talk and share my pain and experiences, to face myself, face myself, face myself. This problem always came up whenever I turned my head.

Face yourself.

'*I can't face myself! Can't face myself!*'

You have no other way.

'*No, I won't do it. I have no one I can hold on to.*'

Hold on to yourself, why are you looking for someone else?

'Why don't you leave me in peace?'

If I leave you in peace, you'll rot.

'Let me rot.'

Why did you come here then? There you were rotting faster than here.

'It was different there.'

If you hold on to yourself, trust in yourself, you'll stop this rot.

'I can't.'

Die, then! What are you waiting for?

For days and weeks I carried on these internal conversations with myself. One side said life, the other said death: they were engaged in a battle of comparisons. Sometimes I would be filled with a terrific wish for life, but it lasted a very short time. I thought I had no right to it. How could I wish for something I had no right to? I had no right to anything. It seemed that I could shoulder any load when I was filled with the wish for life. Then I felt strong.

I needed to start somewhere. But where? How? Yet there were so many people around me who were trying to help.

You have to accept.

'I can't!'

You've got no other choice. If you don't accept that they are there, your experiences, then you can't erase them.

'I can forget them.'

You can't forget them! Months have gone by and you could not forget them, so –

'I'll try harder! I'll forget.'

You'll kill yourself trying.

'No, I'll forget. I'll go on living.'

You're just fooling yourself.

'*No, I'll not accept it, I'll go mad, I'll die.*'

The days came and went. I was fed up, but my comrades, my soulmates, never tired of struggling with me. They kept going on and on and on again.

I had periodic private meetings with Arif who, as ever, talked incessantly and tried to get me to talk too. But I was silent, bowing my head as I listened to him. He spoke of the need to get on my feet again, to become a new person. The two of us had a special rule: I could talk with him at any time and tell him what was on my mind.

But I never did this. He was always the one to request a meeting.

I started writing again in the notebook, but still I did not touch upon much. Around that time a friend wrote me a letter.

'Don't forget to turn your face to the future, towards the dawn – the problems left behind will not be chains on your feet. They are a treasury of past lessons; as you recreate yourself, they will be taken into account.'

To turn one's face to the dawn.

Which way was my face turned? I needed to clarify this. One day I would look towards the dawn, the next I was in darkness.

The days went by swiftly, with no progress. 'I must start somewhere,' I thought, but I wasn't able to take a step and so remained in between death and life. To crawl or to get to my feet? I couldn't go both ways. I had neither the strength nor the confidence. Desperation was eating me up and finishing me off. I wanted to take a step onto the side of life. I used to go up often to that tiny baby. But my feelings of having been dirtied, humiliated and shamed pulled me back. I was headed for the side of death, but the wish for life had caught hold and wouldn't leave me. Both were pulling at me; I felt I would be torn apart.

Hope had come to me the first day I came to Gebze, but I felt I had no right to feel hopeful, so I tried to chase it away, to abandon it; but it, too, stayed the course. Hope and life together.

So where would I start?

The rape. That was the starting point. First, it was necessary to accept that it had happened. When I tried to submerge it, forget it, dismiss it, erase it from my memory, it resurfaced every time to meet me all the more powerfully. It came out while I was sleeping, eating, pacing up and down, watching a film, reading a newspaper or book. Everything, everywhere was conspiring against me. Finally, there was nowhere to run.

'I was raped …' I needed to say this to myself without fear. I tried to say it, but I choked and couldn't take a breath. It wasn't a physical thing. My soul was in great pain. My eyes couldn't see. The tiniest parts of my body were torn, cut, in tatters. I couldn't look in the mirror, at my own face. I felt sick, and vomited. I couldn't even comb my hair in front of a mirror.

When I tried to speak it, the same thing always happened: my tongue and my voice would speak, but my consciousness, mind, heart couldn't accept it.

I was inexorably approaching madness. I struggled with this for weeks. I was still unable to talk to anyone. I hid inside my overwhelming feelings and thoughts.

The date of the trial was now approaching. I had to prepare my statement for the first questioning. Again the question arose as to what I should do. How could I tell my story? I didn't want to say I had been raped. If I did tell, everyone would find out: my mother and father, my brothers and sisters, my husband's family. Everyone would hear. How would I look them in the face? Would they ever be able to look at me and claim me as their own?

One part of me thought it was necessary to tell. After all, I was not to blame. But I had entered a blind alley. These were difficult days. I was torturing myself – I still couldn't take a step.

Finally I decided that I had to tell. Enough! Come what may, I'd had it. I had found myself a second beginning: the trial. Then I broke the promise I myself had implored of Arif. I told others.

No one pressured me to speak about this issue at the trial. They left it to me: 'If you tell, it will be good, but you know best; if you don't want to tell, don't tell.'

I was persuaded by my arguments with friends, but most of all by the outcome of my arguments with myself. It ought not to stay within me, I reasoned. I was not to blame; it was part of the torture.

Meanwhile, my family had secured a lawyer, and I told him everything at our first meeting. He had come on a visiting day, and we met behind a door in a small room. There were other friends' lawyers in that room.

That small room got smaller and smaller. The walls pressed in on me. I felt I would be crushed under them. I couldn't control the shaking in my hands and knees, and I was perspiring heavily. My good friend at Gebze who had previously been in custody with me – she was also named

Gonul – was with me. If she hadn't held my hand, I would have run out of the room. If she hadn't held my hand, I would have run out of the room.

The day of the trial was 8 October. I tossed and turned in bed until morning and awoke as if in a trance. On the one hand I was waiting for the morning to come; on the other, I prayed for the night not to end. I even thought of changing my mind.

That day was not particularly hot, but I was very distressed – my profuse sweating was proof enough for that. Time seemed to stand still. Every second was as long as an age. Every minute I said: 'It's over. I'll die now.'

The courtroom was very crowded. My family, my husband's family and my friends were all there. I began to read my statement, but I couldn't control my voice – I didn't know whether I could be heard or not. I thought the papers would fall out of my hands and then that I'd fall down myself. At one point I saw black and lost my place – it was not I who was reading. At every line I said to myself: 'It's over, now I won't be able to breathe.' I don't know how I finished reading without collapsing; I needed to make an intense effort not to cry when I sat down at the end.

I tried to spot my father among the observers: he was crying. This was the second time I had seen my father cry: the first was at the Security HQ.

I was calm as the prison van returned me to Gebze. I thought I would be relieved, had hoped that the weight on my shoulders would be lighter, but it was the reverse: the burden had increased. But my calmness shocked me; my father's face appeared before my eyes. As soon as I returned to the ward I threw myself on my bed. I was so exhausted, I slept in a semi-coma.

The newspapers carried the news that day and the next. Everyone knew I had been raped – there was no turning back. But I needed to fight even harder against my unwillingness even then to accept the facts. Damn it! My mind and heart were still resisting. With time, though, this resistance weakened. After the truth was out, people's reactions were most important for me. What would they say, how would they look at me, how would they talk? Or would they talk? None of my fears would come true. At the beginning this shocked me. I didn't spot a hint of a negative expression; why weren't people approaching me the way I thought they would?

I found myself being treated in completely the opposite way to what I had imagined. Only a few people had known about my being raped before I had told about it in court, but after that everyone found out. Yet there was absolutely no change in how people treated me beforehand or afterwards, inside the ward or outside. That fact pushed me to cross-examine myself. 'I've experienced torture by rape,' I thought. 'I *must* look upon it as I would suspension torture or beatings.'

I started writing in my notebook more regularly at that time. I wanted to write things that I hadn't told or talked about, but I couldn't do it. For a long time my writing was preoccupied with statements like: 'I've started but I've only got halfway.' It was more about day-to-day details. I was only able to touch on myself a little, but at least I had started. I was able, eventually, to do it, though first I used reading as a means to avoid turning things endlessly around in my head – I still hadn't given up running from myself.

And my nightmares! The nights when I had uninterrupted sleep were few. When I was able to wake up, I couldn't stir in my bed from fear. I either buried my head in the pillow or bit the bedcover. I cried, but didn't want anyone to hear or see me. I suffered from recurring nightmares. For one week, two weeks or longer I would endure the same terrors in my dreamlife.

One nightmare starts beside a stream. All around is bright green; the only sounds come from the stream and the wind in the trees. I am walking: I don't recognise the place from life, but since I have lived through the dream so often it is intensely familiar. I hear sounds, and start walking towards their source. They get steadily closer. Moans, mortal groans and apparitions reach me. Suddenly, hanged people surround me, lynched on trees in the emptiness. They multiply steadily in tens, dozens, hundreds. I can't escape – where would I run to? Whichever way I run I would be faced with hanged people. Women and men, old and young, in the thousands – I can't escape them. I try, but they multiply and I wake up in a sweat.

Another dream has me in the street being chased by two men. I try to take refuge in a house, but I am not able to open the door. As I try, my pursuers wait close by, laughing loudly. Sometimes I manage to get into the house, but it is full of people torn apart: bodies in chunks, arms, legs, heads, all severed but still moving, even laughing and talking; more fleeing and chasing then follow.

I had these nightmares for a long time, beginning in Kirklareli and then in Gebze. I never once had a normal dream in prison.

Shortly after the trial the dreams changed a bit. The hanged people in the emptiness were still there, as were the torn-apart bodies, but they began to speak my name, calling me. A free rope would sway in the emptiness. When I wasn't able to escape, I would reach the rope. I was unable to awaken myself; it was always my friends who woke me.

The thought of death began to preoccupy me intensely. I started thinking seriously that I might have to die. I saw myself as superfluous in this world – I had no place here. I was humiliated, dirtied, my honour tainted. How could such a person have a place in this world?

My friends never left my side. I tried to talk about my feelings but I couldn't say anything. There were limits to what I could say. 'I'm well,' I'd say, 'I'll get over it.' But it was only my tongue that said this. My mind resisted.

They say that death and sleep are twins. When I was in darkness, turned in on myself, choked, sleep was my only shelter. Even if my sleep was broken with nightmares I clung to it, because I had no possibility of thinking when I slept. I was like a corpse.

My attempt to take on the rape and the trial marked a new beginning. After this, my work became a little easier, although it was still extremely difficult.

But I had found the starting point and taken the first step. The rest came more easily.

After I came out into the open in the courtroom, I received so much support from the public. This gave me strength. Every day I received dozens of cards and letters. Those who could came to visit me. My case was championed as a cause by various organisations in campaigns against sexual assault and rape. The cards and letters all said the same thing:

You gave us courage too.

It's not you who should be ashamed, but the perpetrators.
You have taken an honourable step.
You are our honour.

My family and my husband's family never abandoned me. They took me to their hearts from the start. My mother-in-law said. 'Is this not torture?' My sister-in-law agreed. I was most afraid of my father's reaction, that he wouldn't call me his daughter or visit me, whereas in fact my father asked, 'Why didn't you tell me when I came to the Security HQ?' I jumped at the opportunity to embrace him on one of the visiting days, and he kissed me on the forehead.

To them, I was clean, my honour untouched. This made me feel better. But at the same time my self-examination remained difficult. I had got stuck on the honour concept.

What was honour?

After I had spoken out, I found that despite my fears, people did not look on me as a strange, inferior creature or deny me a place among them. I tried to catch a telltale word or look, but I never did, though I was always suspicious. I wondered, were they playing a role? I realised over time how senseless and ridiculous that impression was.

I had been in prison for ten months: five months each in Kirklareli and Gebze. My first New Year in prison came up, and made me sad. The previous New Year felt as though it had occurred only recently – it was just one month afterwards that I was detained. Sometimes I tried to break down the time that had elapsed into seconds, but I couldn't see how the hours, let alone the seconds, had passed.

There was still some distance between the people in the ward and me – I couldn't break that barrier. Nevertheless, after the court appearance I tried to spend more time with them, to join in their conversations and laughter. Around then I received a letter from a friend with whom I'd spent a short time in Bayrampasa. In her letter she asked, 'They say you knit your brows and that your laugh is as depressed as an exiled convict's. Is that true? Why?' I wondered about this. After all, I thought that I had begun to resume laughing.

My husband gave me a jumper as a present for New Year's. I felt strangely upset. I wanted to forget him, not because of any ill feelings towards him but because of my experiences under torture.

As it was the New Year, some short performance sketches had been prepared. I played a small role in one of them, only a one-word part, but I found it very difficult. I just could not get rid of my shame, despite the fact that I knew everyone there, and lived twenty-four hours a day with them.

I continued to try to read books, mostly novels or memoirs. Occasionally I forced myself to discuss what I'd read.

The books I read during that period, fortuitously or not, were all true-life stories from beginning to end. Their heroes had lived through much pain, and those books were written to mark something. What I had gone through was less painful than the lives in those books; I was not the only one in agony. Across the globe, people were experiencing ordeals far crueller than mine. I remember my heart aching when I read *I, Rigoberta Menchú*.

That book is a record of a native Guatemalan woman's experiences. There, children as young as three or four would begin working in the fields. Hunger, poverty and misery followed. Anyone who opposed this way of life was subjected to terrible cruelty. None of the girls from the ages of twelve or thirteen upwards escaped rape by soldiers. As a young girl Rigoberta's elder brother and mother were shot in front of her eyes by soldiers; her mother remained unburied – the soldiers stood guard over the body until it rotted. Parents were tortured to death in front of their children's eyes; they all endured pain and terrible suffering from the day they were born.

The Crazy Birds, *Tamama Pontus's Lost Girl*, *The Resistance War*, *Sweet Orange* and *Olga – Life of a Big-Hearted Girl*: these were all stories of real lives. I realised there were people suffering everywhere: fighting, being raped, tortured, murdered.

There was no other human choice available but to resist. Other people's pain would make me 'get on my feet': I felt this. I had to bandage my wounds as soon as possible, forget my own suffering. Forgetting meant the same as succeeding, as winning.

The books I read, the arguments I had with my dear friends, the dozens of cards and letters in the post every day, all gave me confidence. Most important were the arguments I had with myself. To get back on my feet, to be able to run my life anew, to be able to look myself in the mirror: I now had belief in the possibility of achieving these aims.

What did I argue with myself about?

You've experienced what you've experienced, you can't change that.

'*I know that I have no power to change it, but I have the power to start life anew. I can draw on the lessons of the past and walk into the future. I can turn my face to the dawn.*'

You've looked for a branch to hold on to. Well, have you found it?

'I have, and it wasn't far from me. I can hold on for myself and for the suffering of mankind.'

Haven't you held on to yourself in the past?

'Perhaps so, but there were gaps in the past.'

Aren't there now?

'I can get over them. I can do it. I can get my life running again.'

What about pride, or virtue, or honour?

Now I could not surrender myself to a stupid, warped pride. There were so many people around me who were trying to help; friendly hands, comradely hands. I wanted to hold onto them and never let go. Honour is not in the sexual organs. Honour is in the mind, in the way we live. If I could get over this, life was waiting for me. What could be more honourable than to start life afresh? Now I felt more at ease when I awoke in the morning. The nightmares were becoming less frequent. I felt I was beginning to get pleasure from life. I got pleasure from reading poetry, from making jokes with people and from pacing the ward, playing ball, eating.

But I still tried to keep a distance from everything that would remind me of my experiences. I didn't go to bed before I was quite ready to sleep, as I was alone there and didn't want to think. Thinking brought me back to the past.

The condition I was in during the first days at Gebze came to mind from time to time. I could see the difference. I had a been like a corpse, physically and mentally. I hadn't wanted to live. I was completely shattered psychologically and had been seriously damaged. I recognised the lengths to which my comrades and friends struggled to help me.

Arif, for example, went through the *Turkish Medical Council Journal*. During one of our conversations he told me about a test he'd found in one of them that purported to provide evidence of psychological trauma manifesting after torture. He read out the questions and I gave answers. At first I resisted. 'I'm not ill,' I said. 'I don't need treatment or a doctor, I can get out of this myself.'

The prison garden could be seen from where we were talking. There were a few small trees, and plenty of green. I looked at the garden and said,

'This greenery signifies something to you but means nothing to me.'

Arif suggested I go to the hospital or to a psychologist. At first I refused, but I realised that I wasn't thinking soberly or logically. The only thing I could do was surrender myself to those friends and 'real' people who were holding out their hands. And I did that. I wanted to feel life in the marrow of my bones, I wanted to breathe, to laugh! But I also saw that the longing for death, the hopelessness and helplessness, had not entirely released their grip on me.

I did not think of all this in concrete terms or weigh it up. It happened in a practical way, aimed at regeneration. I listened to a voice:

Rejoin life, get to know it again and like it. Don't live like a child looking out a window but like a child running and playing in the streets, hands all muddy, scrapping and horsing around.

My sources of strength appeared to be inexhaustible. In

whatever direction I turned my head I saw people reaching out with a helping hand. My friends showed that they would be with me to the end, that even if I left them for a time they would not leave me.

But I had to feed the spring within myself. I had to live. I had to call the torturers to account.

I kept up the reading and writing, and even began studying philosophy with Gonul. At first it was difficult. We couldn't understand the material, but we had no intention of giving up. Sometimes we would do crazy things.

The hours in the evening were best for working in the ward. One evening we sat down and really tried to work. But as we were forcing ourselves, it became more difficult, and we got upset. The two of us were trying to work out what we were reading – but in vain! The conversation slid into different subjects without our even noticing it: the meaning of life, our problems, the future. Gonul suddenly began tearing up our study notes. I watched without reacting. She tore them up into bits, and then began to hurl the little pieces of paper into the air.

'What are you waiting for?' she shouted. 'You do it too!'

I hesitated.

'Go on, you throw them too. Don't be afraid. Don't be afraid of yourself or what you want to do.'

'I'm not afraid!'

Then I too started to tear the papers and throw them into the air. We ripped up all the papers we had, then gathered the fallen ones up and threw them around again and again. We watched them drift to the ground. This was a sort of challenge to life from both of us. I felt a release of tension. The two of us laughed so much we cried.

There was no going back, no going halfway. We were going forward, and however slowly, our steps were getting longer.

I didn't miss any of the volleyball matches. Previously, despite really wanting to, I couldn't play and had had to settle for just watching. I also resumed walking in the rain, which I loved to do.

I no longer distanced myself from the other people in the ward, and began to joke with them and wind them up. We were getting ready to put on a play by Yilmaz Erdogan, in which I had a part. I had never done this sort of thing before, apart from a role I had played in primary school and the one sentence in the New Year show.

In this play my part was a long one. I didn't think for a moment as to whether or not I could do it, just agreed to the role and acted it. I was surprised when my friends, who were in charge of getting the play ready, said that during the read-through I was the first person they thought of to play the part.

I played the role of the watchman Murtaza, who had a strong personality. That day many people didn't recognise me. This meant I had taken another step. I was able to face a crowded audience. Despite some anxiety as to whether or not I'd remember my lines or be over-excited, I went out to act.

It was then that I got to know the lines that I have come to love: 'There is no way out/ my heart/ no other way/ we will survive these pains/ because experience is winter.'

At the first trial and all the subsequent hearings my lawyer had made an official complaint on my behalf to bring the police to justice. He insisted that I go to the hospital for treatment, but each time the request was turned down.

The main aim in going to the hospital was to obtain a report on the rape. I had learned that however much time has passed since the occurrence of rape, there are certain tests that could prove it. There was a Psychosocial Trauma Centre at the Capa Medical Faculty. I didn't believe that I was ill, or felt that I needed treatment. We began to shift tactics when the court consistently refused to grant the request. We thought of going to the psychiatric unit of Gebze State Hospital and getting referred to Capa from there. It was a long and troublesome process, but we couldn't find any other way. I spoke a few times to a doctor from the Gebze psychiatric unit. I told the doctor at our first meeting why I had come. I stressed my disturbed sleep and other conditions that were upsetting me. I said forcefully that I needed to go to Capa. The doctor said that this could happen only after a few examinations and he wrote out a prescription. I didn't use the prescription, because I didn't think that I needed treatment or medication. At last I managed to get the referral to Capa.

Since Gebze is in the province of Kocaeli, it is very difficult to get a referral to an Istanbul hospital. The referrals from outside the city take a long time, and I waited for almost two months.

During this period my sleep improved a lot compared with before, and the nightmares disturbed me less.

On 19 June 1998 I was referred to Capa. I continued intermittently to write in my notebook. I wrote the following on the same day:

'Finally I've got the referral to Capa. But why am I afraid?

Will I live through everything again? Damn it! Why don't I fly up into the sky? Why don't I dive into a sleep from which I'll never awaken? Why, why, why? Courage ... Damn it!

'One side is like the dark face of the moon and the other side, the bright face. I am in the light and in the dark at the same time. I can't be free even at the moment I feel most free: am I starting again just when I've finished? Why don't you change your mind? What's holding you? What's binding you?'

The hospital process would make my wounds bleed again, I decided, and I couldn't allow that. I had bandaged and treated these wounds. I wouldn't let them open them again. I had to finish this business really quickly.

My visit to the hospital just about coincided with my husband's birthday, a few days later on 22 June. My notebook entry for that day reads:

'Today it's his birthday. If I were not stuck inside I would give him a bunch of country flowers. This is the second of his birthdays that we are apart. I leafed through the pages for last year and found nothing. Absolutely nothing.

'I have gone through a long, dark tunnel. I think I've come out of that darkness, but it has taken a lot out of me. The ashes are left behind. As I tried to recreate myself from these ashes, even reluctantly, one part of me leaned on you. I reflect often on my feelings for you.

'To breathe on the summits of mountains. To stretch a hand to the sun. To look at the stars, to work incessantly like ants.'

Two weeks later, on 9 July, I wrote this:

'Today was a busy day. I picked flowers from places where flowers can't grow. I gave my face to the sun, the stars and the wind. I scattered to the whole world the flowers I had picked from the mountain peaks. I scattered them so that the children could laugh and play to the fullest. I scattered them so that exploitation and cruelty would vanish from the world.

'And I said to myself never. Once more I said, *never*. "There is no way out/ my heart/ no other way/ we will survive these pains/ we'll walk on fighting and struggling and never ever surrender/ once more ..."'

For 16 July there are only two short entries in the notebook: 'The dreams and nightmares have come back. Will there be no end to them?'

Then I got a letter in the post from a very dear friend:

'Turn your face to the sun, to the future and walk. Walk to win new battles. Walk on in the knowledge that you have gained people's love and fired their anger, and that your name is linked with an honourable and courageous resistance. That bad storm is over, the fog has lifted. Walk on, overcoming the pain before you get used to it. Before you is a future stretching out for you to live as you wish, with your willpower and consciousness, labour, belief and passion and desire for bringing them to account. "Feed the spring inside you" for all of us.'

The first day at the hospital I was calm, so much so that it shocked me. I trusted myself not to lose my calm. I would tell everything soberly, and if I got a report that would be the end of the matter.

It was a beautiful day. On the way I looked out at Istanbul, at the Bosphorus; the ferries; the streets; the crowds; the buses; the men selling bread and fish at Sirkeci; the Besiktas area. Life had continued as I had left it.

As we neared the hospital I got a bit nervous: what would

happen? How would they act? These and similar questions attacked my mind. I had realised one thing: that I would be forced to remember my experiences. There was no sense in forgetting anything. There was no reason to distance myself even a little from life, despite the unbearable pain. I had to prepare myself for this.

I went to my first meeting and a few subsequent ones saying to myself: 'I'll be calm, I'll be dispassionate,' but I couldn't manage it. After a point I said to myself, 'Come on, that's enough! Whatever happens, happens.' I cried as much as I needed to – I didn't try to hold back and couldn't have anyway.

I told the doctor at my first appointment of my experiences and reasons for coming. After a few questions, I began crying as I spoke. I wasn't dismayed – I had expected to do so. Despite the crying, I was calm, and the doctor gave me an appointment for two weeks afterwards. The second meeting was much more detailed. There was a specialist there from the Psychosocial Trauma Section. After this meeting the problems began again – or perhaps they hadn't quite begun then, but that is what I believed at the time. In reality, my problems had been far from overcome; it wasn't a matter of something that had ended starting up again. The specialists conducted tests and asked questions; I talked, remembering details I had no wish to and enduring ghosts emerging one by one. Nevertheless, I insisted on thinking that I didn't need treatment.

There were questions about the rape and questions I thought were very strange and, I felt, irrelevant. The image-association tests struck me as especially strange at the time: there were cards the size of notebooks and on them lots of different, almost meaningless, pictures and drawings. They asked me what I saw in them; answering was like doing a crossword. On my second visit to the hospital I spent the whole afternoon on these tests. But my doctor insisted that no soldiers or warders be present at our meetings; as a result I was able to answer the questions honestly, and was much more at ease.

After the tests the psychotherapy started. At first I just gave very brief answers. They made an effort to get me to tell my story. Eventually I was able to stop holding back. If I didn't tell or share it wasn't likely that they could understand or help me, I reasoned. But it was so difficult to tell certain details that I couldn't find the words or form sentences.

After the second meeting, as a result of what I'd said and told and of the tests, it became clear that I would be prescribed medication. This threw me again, but the situation was very different from that of eight months earlier. Then, my thoughts were far from well, whereas now I was more in charge. There was no reduction in my anxiety and the pain I felt. The pains were still the same pains: it was I who was different.

At the beginning I was against treatment with medication. I thought they would dope me, and I did not want to be tranquillised. If I were to overcome my trauma, I couldn't do it on tranquillisers. But the doctors gave me more information about the medication, and because of their clarifications as to why I needed it, and as a result of my friends' insistence, I agreed. I was also prescribed sleeping tablets, as well as two other pills which had very strong side-effects. Since my constitution was so weak the side-effects were very pronounced in me, despite the fact that the dose was very low.

For a long time I had no problems attending the hospital

appointments. For someone in prison I was lucky enough to get to all of them, whereas for many others it was disturbingly difficult. At last, when the hospital gave me the report, I submitted it to the court; it was accepted as evidence and reported in the press. It was then that the problems began.

After the press broke the story the routine of my visits was broken. I was at the whim of the prison administration, the soldiers and the Ministry. It looked like my appeals to the hospital authorities had achieved good results, but then the arrangements failed again. Whereas before, authorisation from the Ministry covered all visits, I now had to get permission for each appointment. Waiting for official clearance even in urgent cases could take a month and in normal situations a lot longer, whereas my appointments were scheduled at intervals of only fifteen days.

But otherwise I feel I was really lucky: every doctor involved with my case took a close interest in me. They made great efforts to see me on my own. As a result, there were frequent arguments with the soldiers. In the end, I had a run of nine months' treatment in total.

I thought I had secured a good dialogue with each of my three doctors. It was the way they related to me that was significant. From the very first I didn't detect any inclination in them to finish their work in a hurry. On the contrary, they appeared genuinely interested in helping. After I noticed their attitudes my task became a lot easier; it was important that I be made to feel at ease. Whereas at the beginning I had been taking steps backwards, I now started making progress. I had seized on this possibility in prison and I was trying to get value from it, right to the end.

It was a difficult stretch both physically and mentally. I became dependent on the medication, lost my appetite and started losing weight. My already-disturbed sleep became extremely disturbed. Either I wouldn't sleep at all or I'd sleep for eighteen hours non-stop. My nightmares, which had been less frequent, came back with a vengeance. This time they were very different. My experiences at the Security HQ repeated themselves in my sleep. But I also started having more normal and interesting dreams; I started dreaming of everything from political and sports personalities to films and news programmes. I remember seeing Tansu Ciller, the former prime minister; Cakici, the gangster; Sophia Loren; and Kenan Evren, the army commander. Everything I experienced during daytime hours was reflected in my dreams. This was an important change as I hadn't had a normal dream for months. When I awoke I would tell everything about these cinematic dreams that I was able to remember. My dreams were thoroughly discussed for a time on the ward. 'What dreams did you have last night?' became a popular question.

Shortly after I began to use the pills I experienced problems with my balance. I couldn't walk in a straight line; my feet crossed, and I had to hold onto things while walking. Sometimes I fell. Finally my friends refused to leave my side as I fell so frequently, especially when walking down steps. Wherever I went someone was with me. Even while I was sleeping someone was always with me. I started to sleepwalk and talk while asleep as well – I was unable to recall doing these things, but was told so later. I had never at any stage in my life walked or talked in my sleep. After a while, when I awoke I began immediately asking, 'Did I do anything?'

Emine was in the next bunk, and during that period she remembered much clearer what I went through. In her own words:

'You went to bed in the evening and fell asleep. You got up again in your sleep and went towards the kitchen. A friend who was in the ward saw you getting up and walking, not too well, and asked, "Where are you going Asiye? Let me help you." You replied, "Why should you help me? It's I who should help you," you said. So you held on to each other and went down to the kitchen. Other friends in the kitchen sat you on a chair, and you continued to sleep there. Since we knew that if you woke up you could panic at having sleepwalked, we carried you back and laid you on your bed. When you woke up you didn't know what you had done and we made a point of not telling you.

'On 17 or 18 December you stopped your medication. Two days later we noticed that you were trembling intensely from the legs upwards. Before that, when you took the medication regularly there had been no need for alarm. You wanted to stop your medication, but your treatment hadn't finished, so you decided to go off it as an experiment. We struggled with you. You took your daytime medication that evening: two pills, at an interval of forty-five minutes between them. About one hour later you stretched out on the bench in the kitchen and went to sleep there and then. When we realised you were asleep, we said, "Asiye, go to bed now." But you maintained, "No, my grandma is calling me. I'll go to her." We tried to stop you again, and to awaken you ... '

They said that when I talked in my sleep I sometimes made perfect sense. I talked to my grandma – about whom I have not the slightest glimmer of a memory. Emine noted down the following snatches of 'conversation'; I don't remember a single word from them:

'Oh, my God, you've gone, does that mean I have to come too?'

'Grandpa's here beside you. Why are you calling me, you crazy woman?'

'I'll come in thirty or forty years' time; beat it. Look, I'll sing you a song and you'll run away like a lamb.'

'You're dressed all in black – you should wear white. There are *houris* there, aren't there?'

'Eh, leave my grandpa, come here with the *houris*. Go on, leave the man on his own.'

'Eh, darling, you were going to come so often, why have you gone? Was it I who said "go"? Well, I'm not coming. Do they speak in Arabic there?'

'Goodbye, then.'

'How stubborn you are. I said I wouldn't come. *You* come *here*.'

'Is there a lot of traffic there?'

Those were the sorts of conversation that took place. From time to time I tried to walk in my sleep. When people asked me where I was going I answered, 'My grandma is calling me.'

My talks with my grandma, my wanting to be by her side and her calling me all made my heightened sense of death reappear. I was talking to a dead person and wanting to be with her. Why? What was happening? Why didn't the feeling of death go away? What was missing, or was it denial?

When I dreamed certain dreams it wasn't difficult for me to awaken, but I couldn't remember them – these weren't the ones that upset me. It was more the ones wherein I was being chased by certain people who cut my arms and throat, or the ones I had of being raped. When I had these dreams no one could wake me. Sometimes they struggled for one or two hours, but still I wouldn't come to.

One evening I dreamed a faceless man was trying to cut my throat and eventually succeeded. I was later told by my friends that they carried me, half in a faint, half still dreaming, to the exercise yard and made every effort to bring me round. They splashed water on me and made me smell cologne, onions and other unpleasant things. Finally, they called the doctor. I couldn't breathe – I believed my throat had been cut and that I was covered in blood. My friends said they couldn't count the number of times I fainted, but it was probably seven or eight. From time to time it appeared that I had come to, but that all I could see was the blood flowing from my throat. That evening they struggled with me for about four hours. When I awoke the whole ward was by my side. Arif and Hasan had come with the doctor. I couldn't recognise or distinguish the faces of anyone. They didn't leave my side until they were sure that I could recognise them. At the time Gonul and I had been working on the concept of 'denial' in our philosophy course. To make me laugh Arif called me 'Asiye in denial'.

When I revived completely, I was deeply exhausted. I had never drunk milk with sugar, but I didn't say no to it that evening. My blood pressure had dropped by a third. The next day they put me on a serum drip, and only after that was I able to get up and walk around a bit.

Another time I dreamt was in the Security HQ again. One of my best friends who was present describes the incident best:

'You were lying face down or on your side, and your fists

were clenched. We couldn't unclench your hands and you appeared to relive the rape. 'Don't do it, leave me!' you shouted and then screamed. Your whole body was absolutely rigid. Then you fainted again. Again we struggled to wake you. A little later you woke up, but you didn't recognise us – however, you did remember the friend with whom you'd been at the Security HQ. "Last night they put you by me, but then they took you away," you said.

'We told you that had happened two years ago. We tried to tell you to look around, that all that was in the past. We asked about the friends you had known before. "I know they beat him up badly," you said. Another one "couldn't breathe," you said, and started to cry. We told you it had passed, that everything was over and many people had been released. Then from time to time you said: "I want to wash. I've become very dirty." We told you that you were clean, that your bed and bedding were clean too. But you insisted: "No, I'm very dirty, they dragged everything on the ground." We said, "OK, you'll have a wash, let the water heat." But you told us, "I can wash in cold water. My mother's brought some things."

'We tried to bring you back to yourself. You started saying that you were in Gebze, but only because we had told you so. Slowly you started to recognise and remember the people in the ward. You remembered who was on duty and who was making breakfast, but still only agreeing with short answers or sighs. You insisted on washing; then we went to the bathroom. You had a bath in the hot water we had heated. You didn't feel uneasy with us there. You said your shoulder and arm were aching, and asked whether you had been hurt. You preferred water to be poured over you. Then you started crying.

'You rinsed and dried yourself. One of the jumpers we had brought for you to put on was black and the other, which you had taken off, was white. You said you didn't want to put the black one on as it was dirty. You preferred the white one. Then we realised that you still were not conscious of what you were doing. We told you again that everything was in the distant past, that you had gone to court and were attending hospital. You listened to all of this and nodded and accepted it. You said you remembered.

'After you got dressed, we asked if you were OK. You said, "I've dressed right, no one can touch me now." When we asked who touched you, you replied, "Everyone." Again we reminded you that you were in Gebze. After we'd dried your hair we all went to the kitchen for lunch. As we came into the kitchen, you said your head was spinning, and you collapsed, fainted right there and then. After you came round you ate some food, but very reluctantly. It was obvious that you just felt you had to. You were torpid and exhausted. An hour later, while you was sitting by the window a friend warned you, "Don't sit there, you've just had a bath. You'll catch cold." You asked when you had last had a bath, and we told you that you'd just had one. We understood that you hadn't remembered anything.'

Those were difficult days. I was struggling, sometimes second by second. Those days tore me apart. On the other hand, there were days when my hope and belief in the future increased. With great difficulty, I still nurtured the belief that the harsh and extraordinary circumstances of the past were destined to be left behind. In place of resentment I substituted longing and the desire to succeed; in place of pain, anger; in place of sadness, enthusiasm.

The coming and going to and from the hospital turned into a torture. I'd return from there and throw myself on my bunk just as I was, exhausted by the journey but more from the heavy talking I had had to do.

I would go to sleep and every time have terrible nightmares. Or I wouldn't sleep at all. Once I returned from the hospital and couldn't sleep. It was nighttime and everyone in the ward, except for a couple of people, was asleep. I was suffocating – I had to talk to someone. It wasn't important what I said, I just had to have someone listen to me. I had to cast off the distress within me, or else I wouldn't know what I'd do or what would happen to me. I was afraid that I would spin out of control. I went downstairs, had a cigarette, then went upstairs again. I went down again, back up, down again, up again. In the end I woke up Gonul.

'Gonul,' I said, and her eyes opened immediately. She got up straightaway and we went downstairs. Now I laugh when that scene comes to mind. All that day I had struggled with Gonul and didn't leave her in peace for a second. She must have thought she would have been clear of me at night. I said, 'I'm going to tell you the story of my childhood. She replied, 'OK', and I talked for hours, with no silences. At times we laughed and laughed.

I told her whatever I remembered about my childhood, whatever sprang to mind that was connected with it. At the age of five or six we moved from Dolapdere to Aksaray, and lived there for almost a year. My mother took my sister and me in the afternoon to the Aytekin Kotil Park, which was near our house. I talked for hours but I only succeeded in recounting my life and times until that point. Friends of ours were working at night in the mess hall, and Gonul and I had to go somewhere else so as not to disturb them, as we were laughing so much. The hours of talking made me feel better and also made me tired.

Later the Aytekin Kotil Park story became a great source of laughter. The next time I went to the hospital I got the opportunity to see this park from the prison van as we passed Aksaray. On my return everyone was waiting expectantly for me to recount what had taken place at the hospital, but I said, 'Gonul, do you know they've turned half of Aytekin Kotil Park into a market?'

At these moments, however many people are around you, however much help they try to give, the awareness sets in that the one who has been diagnosed is you. It was I who was feeling the pain, I who was torn apart, I whose heart ached so much it was difficult to describe.

I didn't know what effect the medication was having on me, and I didn't feel the need to ask. Instead, several times I asked the doctors: 'Am I ill?' They gave me a very straight answer: 'You're asking, "am I mad?"; in fact, that's something else altogether. But you do have a mental illness, damage as a result of your experiences, and that needs to be treated.'

What could I say? The doctors were medical experts in all sorts of fields. At the first two meetings, the tests were directed at determining what I was suffering from. I answered hundreds of questions, and every question opened another wound.

After the second meeting I realised that I had a clear-cut decision to make. Either I would finish this business within the allocated time span or I would continue to play this game of hide-and- seek with myself. If I preferred the latter it would mean that I would live with this suffering all my life, surrender to the sufferings and continue to be torn apart. But how far would I flee and where would it end? My answer to that question was not very attractive: the grave.

A volcano continues to burn deep inside during even the quietest moments. When it gets to the point of explosion, no force can stop it. It burns every possible thing around to ashes, swallows up everything in its path. That terrifying force that mounts inside calms down only when the flames are expelled.

The human heart is like a volcano; but this heart, when it doesn't unburden itself or is unable to share the things within it, causes only damage to itself. The pressure builds gradually and erupts. But whereas a volcano destroys everything outside itself, the heart controls nothing in the outside world. Its eruption is like pulling the pin of a grenade held in your hand – you destroy yourself.

'I must feed the spring within me, I must live, must call them to account for my experiences.' This was my jumping-off point. I thought that just by repeating this, everything would be OK.

I continued insistently to run away from myself. I still didn't come to terms with my past, or try to extract lessons from it. I took the attitude only that what I'd lived through, I'd lived through, and now I had to look to the future. I had calmed the storm in my heart, but done only that, and not reduced the origins of the storm. My heart had calmed down, but the slightest breeze would disturb the waters and dark black clouds would descend on me.

My decision came down not on the side of the grave, but on the side of living. I was conscious that the next period would be much harder than the previous one, and that is in fact what happened, but this time I was much stronger, more decisive. I wouldn't ever get used to past suffering; I would overcome it. 'There is no way out/ my heart/ no other way/ we will survive these pains': These lines were on my mind at every moment. I was no longer helpless, having even achieved the confidence and the good poise necessary for cultivating high hopes.

But my nightmares still had not stopped. It was difficult to free myself from their influence, however I might try. I sweated and struggled. My usual way of dealing with them had been to cry and wait for them to go. What had I not done? I decided that the moment I came round, I would say whatever came into my mind – it didn't even need to make sense. I talked instantly, because of my desire to emerge from the effects of the dream. The topics included people, incidents, the television news or scenes from the cinema.

One day as I was trying to emerge from the effects of a dream, an article which I'd read in a magazine the previous day was the first thing that came to mind.

The article was about cicadas and ants. Cicadas stay under the earth for fourteen or fifteen years, then at the end of that stretch they resurface and must find a mate within two weeks or die; and they sing to attract a mate, rubbing their wings together an impossible number of times per second. There were also some details on the life of ants. When I came to I began to speak of these things. The faces of the people who were trying to wake me were uncomprehending. I can laugh now when I think of their disbelieving expressions, but at the time I wasn't in a condition to do so. They assumed I'd had a dream about such things , but my aim was to calm down as soon as possible and emerge from the destructive effect of the dream I did have. If I did not calm myself, I couldn't tell how long the effect of the dream would last: one or two days, or even a week.

Books continued to sustain me. I read in bed for hours; I read the classics at this point in time. My hobbies also multiplied: I started knitting and painting pottery vases that my sister brought from Nevsehir. I did these things when most distressed, struggling to reduce the pain and firing myself up for a terrible fight. People said this was reflected in my work. I had to be merciless with myself. If I pitied myself I could find a whole series of excuses – 'if this had happened that would have happened or couldn't have happened', etc. If I took the road of self-pity I wouldn't have been able to use my willpower.

Sometimes I forgot how to laugh. When I lost my sense of humour, fear invaded me from all sides. There's a Kazakh saying: 'A soul that writhes in fear erases thought from the mind.' Not to see the reality of a situation is the road to destruction, whereas my aim was to throw out any destructive thing and be stronger than the past. I had to accept my own reality, but I didn't accept that I was destroyed and didn't reconcile myself to the situation.

I got the opportunity to argue many issues with my doctors. At the beginning it was only they who did the talking or asked the questions. I made do with short answers. But then I noticed that I felt better when I talked.

To share without hiding anything, to tell what I needed to helped me regain control of myself. I started trusting myself again. This proved a key point in making me face myself. It was what made me able to look at my future without fear.

At this time I was called as a witness in a torture case that had been brought by friends with whom I had been charged. I had obtained the report from the hospital, but no court case had yet been brought against me. This trial was very important from my point of view – I would face my torturers. Almost one and a half years had gone by, but I would come up against those who had put me through the heaviest pain. I was excited, distraught, tense. My balance problems continued. As this first confrontation approached my nerves became more and more tense. My calm had flown out the window at precisely the moment when I most needed it.

Representatives from the big pro-democracy organisations, our families and the press were all there. The courtroom was crowded, and the police were there in full force in the corridor and sitting in the front row of the hall. I was shown to a seat close to them but I didn't, couldn't, sit there. I was incredibly afraid that I wouldn't keep calm. Since I was a witness they took me to another room with a soldier on either side of me.

The clock stopped, time stood still. Finally I was called into the courtroom. Many of the torturers I knew were there.

I tried to tell of my experiences and what I had seen. I had a lump in my throat and couldn't speak as I wanted to. I couldn't stand it when the judge asked a particular question and I started crying. Damn it, I thought, I must be calm, but I couldn't be! I had seen them, had looked at their faces.

But I had been able to look them in the face!

Resistance, hope, willpower ... there were no other choices for me. Was I strong enough to use my willpower? What had I done in a year and a half – had I taken steps, and if so, what steps? What had I done to make myself a new person, to remove the damage, to get on my feet?

The most difficult part for me, of course, had been to reveal that I had been raped in custody. After revealing that, there was no going back. I had been able to do this, and no one had forced me – in fact they had even reassured me that I needn't say anything. I had made the final decision and come out with it. If I hadn't, what would have happened? My experiences would have just stayed within me and I would have spent the rest of my life in shame and disgust. It wasn't I who should have been ashamed. I had been tortured, beaten and raped! But why *was* I ashamed?

And hadn't I known of these things? I knew, had heard and read about them. I knew that one day, as an opponent of the regime and as a socialist who insisted on her identity, that one day I would be tortured. I had had long conversations with several people on this issue. I had also spoken with my husband about torture and rape. Several books I had read and articles in newspapers showed that rape in custody is used in nearly every country in the world as a method of systematic torture. It wasn't a method of torture aimed only at women, but also at men. But I believe it damages women to a greater extent, and this fact is used by the police to achieve results. I knew all this, but still I was ashamed – always at the thought of my friends, husband, mother, father, brothers, sisters.

Why? Why was I ashamed? I hadn't done anything wrong. What I had done was to come out against social injustice and cruelty. I lived in a country where injustice and all kinds of cruelty are rife. I considered it my duty as a human being to come out against these things. My shame wasn't from this, there was something else. What was it?

Honour? Was my honour stained because I couldn't protect my sex? Or, hadn't I defended the values I believed in strongly enough? How about my husband? Was my honour defiled for him? Why did I see myself as his honour? Why did I think he'd never touch me again? I wasn't to blame. And why did I look for blame in myself? I didn't think that when I was naked and suspended. Why did I think like that now? It was systematic and conscious torture.

These questions followed one after another. I was fighting with myself, I had answers to give and answers that I feared to give and that wouldn't emerge. But I would overcome all the barriers one by one. I was in charge of myself and of my suffering; I had taken control. The rest was a question of work and time.

Strength is consciousness, strength is in knowing what you want and loving it with a passion.

Loneliness starts when you decide that there are things you can't share with the person closest to you. Round about you there may be hundreds of people, but this is no obstacle to your being lonely. The moment you decide you can't share, you begin to flee from yourself, to live as a stranger to yourself – a torn-apart personality.

You think you are the centre of your life, whereas in fact it is not like that; while there are people around you, you are strong. I had thought that I was strong. But when I was truly alone I saw that I was not. You are alone when you are tortured. You are alone when you are suspended, you are alone when you are beaten. Your eyes are blindfolded for twenty-four hours at a time. You are lonely; you are not allowed to speak with anyone; you must ask permission to go to the toilet; you are kept standing and waiting. The black blindfolds are put on when you are taken into custody and they are only taken off at the toilet door for you. Apart from these moments you are in darkness. You can only tell whether it's night or day from the movements around you. You can only give answers to the people who ask the questions – otherwise it's forbidden to talk. You are made lonely and alone.

At such a moment you need to engage your consciousness and your heart. If your feelings and thoughts are united, then you are made strong. Under your feet the mountains, the forests, the oceans are spread out; the faces you love smile. But if your feelings and thoughts are different to each other, these conversations will make you lonelier. You'll seek but you will not find, you'll call and shout; no voice will answer. The only conversation you can have is with your heart and your torturers. If you are not whole, if your consciousness is split, then your second 'I' will begin speaking to you.

This 'I' talks and does not leave you in peace. It is always against you, and makes you do things that you don't want to do. You can't prevent it, nor can you shut it up – because it is powerful at such a time. It's been suppressed, hidden, but it surfaces in its most powerful form at the most difficult moments. It compels you to do what it wants, and you finally become the 'you' inside of you. You do everything it wants you to do; you sign any papers put in front of you – it's not important what's written on them.

I used to always believe while on the outside that I was strong, that I could shoulder my burdens, that nothing would destroy me – but then I was so destroyed that it was difficult to return.

I was not a single person when I was taken into custody, when I was blindfolded, when I was tortured, when I was raped. The other 'I' was talking to me nonstop. I couldn't shut her up; I tried to chase her away, but she was too strong. I hadn't been able to notice her in my former life, or she hadn't been visible. She only really came out when I was alone. But I always suppressed her, though she urged, 'count me in, consider me'. I didn't consider her.

Now I notice her, and am conscious of this quality: a person's willpower is their most powerful weapon. There is no obstacle outside any person that stops one starting a new life, because human beings really do carry within them a superbly resilient life-force.

Formerly I leaned on everyone except myself. I couldn't realise my strength. I kept seeking a place to lean on. Why didn't I notice myself. Was I that weak?

Why did I feel the need to lean on anyone? I didn't want to believe I was that weak. My powerlessness was out in the open. I had collapsed when I was left on my own, and dragged along the ground. My own heart had turned away from me.

But like all people, I had a hidden power that needed to come out into open. I had to learn to stand on my own, to live for myself, not for others.

The war of a person with themselves is the most difficult. We don't want to accept the negative things, but to be perfect, open, loyal – as though raised in another world. But this never reflects the real state of affairs. I realised that I was nailed to the bottom of the abyss. I saw the real 'I' inside me, and I was afraid. I tried to flee and I did flee, but in the end there was nowhere left for me to go. In the end I was left face-to-face with my own reality in all its mercilessness. Well, then, I had to learn to be merciless. These qualities were within me, and I had carried them for years.

I couldn't reject the unwavering support of my friends. What was important, however, was that was that I asked for as well as welcomed it. This was also true of the care of the doctors who had treated me. My aim became clearer at each meeting. I was becoming free to continue on my way, to feel the spring; to sense the sun, the stars, the moon; to hear the sounds of rivers, oceans, forests; to hear the voices of people and children. I learned to want to feel my pain. One cannot treat a wound one can't see.

To want and to love. This was the key. But I had to demonstrate this not just in words but in action. First I had to love: life, people, myself. When I said 'I want', I couldn't retire to a corner. I couldn't wait for happiness to come up to me. Only by wanting it could I find it.

It was important that I did not distance myself from daily life, from which I had cut myself off for so long. I tried to fill the emptiness with books, and indeed, every book I read took me to another world: I wandered around Russia and France in *War and Peace*, and around Paris with *Les Misérables*, Valjean's suffering deeply felt in me. I read about the Native Americans and the splendours of their cultures, fighting with them against genocide. In *Germinal* I was on the side of the mineworkers. I fought at Stalingrad, and against the Nazis with the Resistance. I was together with those fighting against Fascism in Germany. I went to Latin America.

I'd come to know the world, and that my suffering and joys alike mirrored the experiences of millions of people in the world. I was not alone, nor did the world revolve around me.

Thus I filled my life with every colour I perceived, even black, which I had avoided because it so evoked the abyss. But I later added it as well; if life was to be whole, all of nature's colours must be present.

One sentence from a book I read caught my attention:

'Withdrawing is not fleeing. It is war's most difficult strategy. Not everyone can withdraw successfully ...'

This was written about Moscow's resistance to the German occupation. I likened my hospital period to this sentiment. I had withdrawn, but even alone in my bunk I held out hope. I had wanted to stay on my own so I could fight more mercilessly. This turning in on myself carried a risk, but I tried to share it. When I did want to talk, my friends were by my side; when I couldn't sleep there were comrades to whom I did not have to hesitate to write to of my feelings. I had withdrawn from daily life, but hope, belief, courage and love warmed my heart.

I destroyed a city in me that I had tried to build and create for years. Then I began to rebuild it, sharing the work, overcoming the solitude. If I hadn't done so, the walls I erected around me would have become too high, and asphyxiated me between them. There would have been no future.

Now the future is redeemed, and I want that future. The torturers will lose. I have complete faith in that. So I shout: *I want the future, I want the future, I want the future!*